The Crimson Book of Highwaymen

THE CRIMSON BOOK
OF
HIGHWAYMEN

Peter Newark

Jupiter Books: London

First published in Great Britain in 1979 by
JUPITER BOOKS (LONDON) LTD
167 Hermitage Road, London N4 1LZ.

Copyright © Peter Newark 1979.

ISBN 0 906379 15 6

Composed in 12-point Monotype Goudy Old Style,
Series 291, by Ronset Limited, Darwen, Lancashire.
and printed and bound in Great Britain.

FOR OLIVE
WHO HELPED ME

Contents

Author's Note

IN RELATING THE STORIES of celebrated highwaymen I have concentrated first on the English variety, followed by their cousins-in-crime, the 'bushrangers' of Australia and the 'road agents' and railway bandits of America's Wild West, a cavalcade of highway robbery starting in the mid-seventeenth century and ending in the early years of the twentieth century.

In writing this volume I have consulted many books and journals and hereby acknowledge my debt to other authors. For readers who wish to pursue this fascinating subject further, a select bibliography of the best and most easily obtained works appears at the end of the book.

PETER NEWARK

Brentwood, Essex, 1979

Note on the Illustrations

ALL THE ILLUSTRATIONS in this book, except the few which carry specific credits, are from the author's own collection. These illustrations are available to picture researchers and publishers from THE HISTORICAL PICTURE SERVICE 86 Park Road, Brentwood, Essex CM14 4TT, England.

PROCLAMATION
$5,000⁰⁰

REWARD

FOR EACH of SEVEN ROBBERS of THE TRAIN at WINSTON, MO., JULY 15, 1881, and THE MURDER of CONDUCTER WESTFALL

$ 5,000.00

ADDITIONAL for ARREST or CAPTURE

DEAD OR ALIVE
OF JESSE OR FRANK JAMES

THIS NOTICE TAKES the PLACE of ALL PREVIOUS REWARD NOTICES.

CONTACT SHERIFF, DAVIESS COUNTY, MISSOURI IMMEDIATELY

T. T. CRITTENDEN, GOVERNOR
STATE OF MISSOURI
JULY 26, 1881

CHAPTER ONE

Heyday of Highwaymen

THE ENGLISH HIGHWAYMAN of the eighteenth century is an immediately recognizable figure, so well-defined has his person and character become over the last 200 years. Mounted on a fine horse, high-booted and spurred, he wears the dark clothes and rakish tricorn hat of a gentleman rider. A black mask or handkerchief covers his face. Armed with a heavy flintlock pistol he commands a coach on a lonely road to 'Stand and deliver!'

He then proceeds to rob the travellers with courtesy and consideration, with particular regard for any ladies present – for he is a gentleman bandit, a 'knight of the road', a member of the criminal élite, and would never descend to the bad language and violence perpetrated by the lowly, pedestrian footpad. Having 'eased' his victim of their valuables and money, the mysterious gallant gives a sweeping bow to the ladies and gallops off in the moonlight . . .

> And he rode with a jewelled twinkle,
> His pistol butts a-twinkle,
> His rapier hilt a-twinkle,
> Under the jewelled sky.
> (From *The Highwayman* by Alfred Noyes)

A legendary figure, yes, but one rooted firmly in fact, albeit embellished to an incredible degree in romantic fiction. In truth there were a number of gentleman highwaymen 'forced' to take to the road for one reason or another, who were celebrated in their own time; indeed, James MacLaine, hanged in 1750, was known as 'the Gentleman Highwayman'. Other mounted thieves, if not of gentle birth,

'Stand and deliver!' An eighteenth century highwayman holds up a lone traveller on Hounslow Heath.

[15]

assumed the mantle and manners of well-born blades. However, there were a great many more highway robbers who held-up travellers at gunpoint with a searing mouthful of abuse, threats, and physical violence. We shall meet them all, gentlemen and blackguards, in the following pages.

Highway robbery flourished in England, as in no other country, during the seventeenth and eighteenth centuries. The heaths and commons around London and the great roads throughout the country were infested with highwaymen and footpads. Even the main streets of London were not safe, nor the monarch's own person secure from robbery. George I, who reigned from 1714 to 1727, was confronted by a highwayman as he walked one evening in his garden at Kensington. Having climbed over the royal wall, the bandit, 'with a manner of much deference', deprived his king of purse and watch.

Why this state of lawlessness? During the heyday of highwaymen, from 1650 to 1800, England was the only civilized nation without a professional police force. Other European countries had military patrols to protect the roads, or a national *gendarmerie* to keep law and order. But the independent, freedom-loving Englishman, or so it was argued at the time, regarded the establishment of a permanent police force as a threat to his individual liberty. More to the point, or to the pocket, there was the high cost involved in maintaining such a force. Anyway, the English did not want 'foreign' ideas imposed upon them.

Thus central government did little or nothing to protect the public from criminal depredations, apart from maintaining small, localized bodies of peace officers such as the city marshals, constables, beadles, and the watch, the latter being ineffectual old men. The officers were mostly corrupt and in this situation of weak law enforcement, citizens were expected to fend for themselves, and to chase and capture villains by hue and cry, the old common-law process of pursuing 'with horn and with voice'. Private enterprise in law enforcement gave rise to thief-takers who hunted down criminals for the monetary reward. The Highwayman Act

[16]

of 1692 established a reward of £40 for the capture and successful prosecution of a highway robber. Jonathan Wild, the most successful of thief-takers, was also the greatest criminal in the land.

With highwaymen 'as common as crows' no honest citizen rode alone, or travelled at night if he could avoid it. He might join a company of travellers, or ride with the long string of pack-horses which still carried goods across country well into the latter part of the eighteenth century,

'Your money or your life!' A
highwayman of the ruffian type
demands his toll from startled
travellers.

or he might travel in the stage-wagon, a huge vehicle which
crawled through the country at a foot-pace and took weeks
upon a journey. Fast stage-coaches flying over good roads
did not come till the late seventeenth century.

To travel, say, from London to Exeter or York was considered a hazardous undertaking, an adventure fraught with
peril and the traveller often made his will before starting

[18]

and took solemn farewell of his family and friends as one who might never see them again. Travellers, especially the wealthy, armed themselves and their servants as if 'going into battle'. When Mrs Calderwood of Coltness travelled from Edinburgh to London in 1756 she recorded in her diary that she carried in her own postchaise a brace of pistols and was escorted by 'John Rattray, my stout serving man on horseback with pistols in his holsters and a good broad sword by his side'.

Highwaymen apart, travel was difficult and dangerous enough because of the awful condition of the unpaved roads, if roads they could be called. In his *Dissertation Concerning the Present State of the High Roads in England, Especially those near London*, published in 1736, Robert Phillips described the wretched condition of the highways: 'In Summer the roads are suffocated and smothered with dust; and towards the Winter, between wet and dry, there are deep ruts full of water with hard dry ridges, which make it difficult for passengers [in coaches] to cross by one another without overturning; and in Winter they are all mud.' Also in 1736, writing from Kensington, Lord Hervey complained, 'The road between this place and London is grown so infamously bad that we live here in the same solitude as we should do if cast on a rock in the middle of the ocean; and all Londoners tell us there is between them and us a great impassable gulf of mud.'

The heyday of highwaymen began with the end of the English Civil War between the forces of Parliament and Charles I. With the king defeated and executed and the Commonwealth established, many Royalist officers found themselves ruined and *persona non grata*. Dispossessed of their estates and properties they took to the road in order to sustain themselves, most of them preying only on the hated Roundheads (Chapter 3: Crooked Cavaliers). These well-bred soldier/outlaws, mounted on blood horses and attired in Cavalier costume set the pattern for the traditional 'knight of the road' and the mounted highwayman came to be regarded as the noblest of criminals.

[19]

To beg is base, as base as pick a purse;
To cheat, more base of all theft – that is worse.
Nor beg nor cheat will I – I scorn the same;
But while I live, maintain a soldier's name.
I'll purse it, I, the highway is my hope;
His heart's not great that fears a little rope.
(*The Cashiered Soldier*, 1643)

As the seventeenth century drew to a close, highwaymen of every stripe infested the land. All a bold and desperate man required was a horse and a pistol and he was in business. He either worked alone or in a band. There was plenty of money to be had on the road. Travel may have been arduous and dangerous but people had by necessity to get about. Wealthy gentlemen travelling between town and country houses, middle-class merchants, farmers returning from market with gold in their pockets, even pedlars with not much to rob, all fell foul of the dreaded commands 'Stand and deliver' and 'Your money or your life'. A typical newspaper report of the time appeared in the *London Gazette* of 1684;

'On Whitsunday in the evening was committed a great robbery by four highway-men within half a mile of Watford Gap in the county of Northampton, to the value of above eight score pounds taken from some passengers. They [the highwaymen] were of indifferent stature, their coats were all turned up with shag [cloth with a long coarse nap], one had a blew shag and wore a perriwig, the others wore their own hair; they had two bay naggs [*sic*], a bay mare somewhat battered before, and a sprig tail sorrel mare, which they took away from one they robbed, and a black nag; one of them had short holsters to his saddle . . . another, a pair of pistols in his saddle cover. Whoever gives notice of the said robbers to Joshuah Snowden, confectioner at the Bellsavage Gate on Ludgate Hill, or to Henry Keys at Watford Gap Inn, shall be well rewarded.'

Plagued as he was by these parasites of the road, the Englishman generally viewed the more celebrated highway-

men with admiration. The Abbé le Blanc, during his travels
through England in 1737, was always meeting Englishmen
'who were no less vain in boasting of the success of their
highwaymen than of the bravery of their troops. Tales of
their cunning and generosity were in the mouths of every-
body, and a noted thief was a kind of hero.'

The highwayman as public hero has been much written
about. Thomas de Quincey (1785-1859) came to the con-
clusion that the profession of highwayman 'required more

[21]

accomplishments than either the bar or the pulpit, since it presumed a bountiful endowment of qualifications: strength, health, agility, and excellent horsemanship ... The finest men in England, physically speaking, throughout the last [eighteenth] century, the very noblest specimen of man, considered as an animal, were the mounted robbers who cultivated their profession on the great roads. When every traveller carried firearms the mounted robber lived in an element of danger and adventurous gallantry.'

Thomas Babington Macaulay (1800-59) stated in his *History of England* that 'It was necessary to the success and even to the safety of the highwayman that he should be a bold and skilful rider, and that his manners and appearance should be such as suited the master of a fine horse. He

Some highwaymen operated alone or in pairs, while others preferred to work in gangs.

[22]

When travellers refused to stop when commanded by highway robbers, the mounted thieves would probably bring down the lead horse.

therefore held an aristocratical position in the community of thieves, appeared at fashionable coffee houses and gaming houses, and betted with men of quality on the race ground. Sometimes, indeed, he was a man of good family and education. A romantic interest, therefore, attached and perhaps still attaches, to the names of freebooters of this class. The vulgar [public] eagerly drank in tales of their ferocity and audacity, of their occasional acts of generosity and good nature, of their amours, of their miraculous escapes, and of their manly bearing at the bar [of justice] and in the [execution] cart.'

De Quincey and Macaulay were, of course, writing in retrospect, in an orderly time when the golden age of highwaymen had long gone. Sir John Fielding, the Bow

[23]

All travellers, wealthy and humble, fell foul of the highwaymen who took their money where they could.

'The pilfered yield no pelf', from a painting by Bernard Munns. A highwayman comes upon a carriage already plundered.

Street Magistrate who had to deal with a continuous flow of highway robbers through his court, had a different view of the highwayman as hero. In 1773 he wrote to Garrick the actor asking him to suppress the popular *Beggar's Opera*, which he produced. Fielding held the opinion that the exploits of Macheath, the highwayman hero, and the glorification of the criminal life on the stage, were calculated to enlarge the ranks of the real highwaymen from the scatter-brained and stage-struck apprentices of the city.

The civil behaviour of the best of English highwaymen greatly impressed foreign visitors, accustomed as they were to rough, ungallant treatment from their own coarse breed of road robbers. Johann Wilhelm von Archenholz, the German historian, observed that English highwaymen were 'generally very polite; they assure you they are very sorry that poverty has driven them to that shameful recourse, and end by demanding your purse in the most courteous manner'. The Frenchman César de Saussure noted that 'some highwaymen are quite polite and generous, begging to be excused for being forced to rob, and leaving passengers the wherewithal to finish their journey'.

These personal observations of the gentle *modus operandi* of the criminal élite are confirmed by many newspaper reports. An example is the following item from the *Birmingham Gazette* of 6 May 1751; 'On Tuesday last, the Shrewsbury caravan was stopped between the Four Crosses and the Welsh Harp by a single highwayman who behaved very civilly to the passengers, told them that he was a stranger in distress, and hoped that they would contribute to his assistance. On which each passenger gave him something, to the amount in the whole of about four pounds, with which he was mighty well satisfied, but returned some halfpence to one of them, saying he never took copper.'

However, while there were a number of well-behaved 'Gentlemen of the Road', there were a great many more who were base and brutal to their victims, men and women alike. Some beat, whipped, and killed the travellers who fell into their grasping hands. When a woman victim had

[25]

Two lone highwaymen meet unexpectedly. On such an occasion they might have joined forces to hold up a coach.

Gentlemen of the Road were great gamblers and attended cock fights, horse races, and the gaming rooms of high society.

trouble in removing a diamond ring, highwayman Tom Wilmot cut off the woman's finger. Many a randy robber seized the opportunity while on the job to satisfy his sexual desire. Captain Zachary Howard not only plundered the house of General Fairfax, but also raped Lady Fairfax and her daughter. When Dick Turpin and his gang raided the house of a farmer, one of the ruffians ravished the maid.

Captain Charles Johnson in his *General History of the Most Famous Highwaymen* (1734) tells us that Jacob Halsey prefaced his rape of a young woman, thus; 'My pretty lamb, an insurrection of an unruly member obliges me to make use of you; therefore I must mount thy alluring body, to the end that I may come into thee.' Patrick O'Bryan, described as 'Murderer, incendiary, ravisher, and highwayman', on taking a fancy to the daughter of a wealthy victim, announced to his confederates, 'Before we tie and gag this pretty creature, I must make bold to rob her of her maidenhead.'

Having resigned themselves to the inevitability of highway robbery, travellers resorted to various tricks to deceive the thieves. A favourite device was to keep a small amount of money in a purse and conceal the major part about their person – in their shoes, stitched into clothing, in a false lining of a hat, in a secret pocket, etc. The purse would be readily delivered to the highwayman, who, if the victim were fortunate, would just curse at the small amount and not bother to carry out a time-consuming personal search.

In 1793 Mr Burdon, a London banker travelling to Durham in a postchaise on urgent business, was stopped by highwaymen and handed over his purse containing twenty-five guineas. The robbers, well-satisfied with the tidy amount, rode off and left Mr Burdon to continue his journey, with 25,000 guineas – destined for a Durham bank – hidden under his seat! Surely the biggest haul so narrowly missed by English highwaymen.

Not all travellers submitted meekly. Some stalwart spirits refused to be intimidated and struck back. Lord Berkeley was a fine example. On a November night in 1774

[27]

he was travelling in his carriage across Hounslow Heath when a commanding voice called upon his driver to halt. The vehicle stopped; a masked man rode up and thrust his pistol through the window at Lord Berkeley, who immediately seized the barrel and turned it away, at the same time he pushed a carbine against the man's body and fired. The robber rode off some fifty yards and dropped dead. His two accomplices fled instantly.

Four main highways led to London and each had its particular black spots, or places of robbery greatly favoured by highwaymen. Hounslow Heath on the Great Western Road was notorious for its criminal activity. It was nothing unusual for noblemen, returning from a visit to the king at Windsor Castle, to be stopped and robbed while crossing the heath. And it was here that Claude Duval, that paradigm of the romantic highwayman, danced an elegant coranto with the lady companion of a gentleman victim.

On the Great North Road, Finchley Common was the popular haunt of highwaymen, including the famous Dick Turpin. Even fifty years after Turpin's execution, the common was a place of dread. In 1790 the Earl of Minto, travelling the road to London, wrote to his wife that instead of pressing on to the city at night, he would wait until morning, 'for I shall not trust my throat on Finchley Common in the dark'. Highwayman Peter Curtis is said to have buried £1,500 on the common, but, apparently, it was never found.

The Dover Road had two infamous spots; Gad's Hill and Shooter's Hill, the former being noted for its robbers long before the seventeenth century. When highwaymen were executed they were usually hung in chains on the scene of the crime (Chapter 2: The Gallows and the Gibbet). Samuel Pepys wrote in his diary that on 11 April 1661 he rode along the Dover Road 'under the man that hangs upon Shooter's Hill, and a filthy sight it is to see how his flesh is shrunk to his bones'. The fourth major highway, the Oxford Road, was saddled with Shotover Hill of bad repute. Here it was that John Cottington, known as 'Mulled Sack',

Travellers resorted to various tricks to deceive the robbers. A favourite device was to keep a small amount of money in a purse and the major part concealed about your person. The purse was readily handed over.

robbed the army pay wagon of £4,000.

Other places notorious for highwaymen activity were Wimbledon Common, Blackheath, Barnes Common, and Bagshot Heath. Salisbury Plain was also noted for its mounted marauders. Here is a report from the *Salisbury Journal* of 24 December 1777: 'HIGHWAY ROBBERY. Whereas Thomas Fowle of Devizes in the County of Wilts was attacked on Monday afternoon on the Plain near the 11 mile stone by two highwaymen, who robbed him of five guineas and a half and his watch . . . The two men were well mounted on dark brown horses, one of the horses had both hinder heels white; they both had surtout [tight-fitting, broad-skirted outer] coats on and appeared to be lusty men. He who robbed Mr Fowle was about five feet ten inches high and was booted and spurred. Whoever will give notice so as one or more of the above highwaymen may be apprehended, shall on conviction receive five guineas

[29]

Stage-coaches were first used to
carry the mail in 1734.

reward over and above the £40 allowed by Act of Parliament, to be paid by me. THOMAS FOWLE.'

The public stage-coach made its first appearance in 1658. The journey was divided into stages, at the end of every stage fresh horses were waiting to pull the coach. The journey from London to York could be made, in fair going, in four days at a cost of £2 per passenger. Stage-coaches were first used to carry the mail in 1734. Before then the mail had been carried by mounted postboys who were unreliable, slow, and vulnerable to robbers. The mail coach brought a vast improvement to the postal service. The mail-bags, which often contained valuables, banknotes and bills were transported with far greater speed and safety, being placed in the care of a well-armed guard.

Gangs of highwaymen attempted to hold up the express mail-coaches and fierce struggles ensued. Sometimes the guard, the coachman, and resolute passengers repelled the bandits; sometimes the robbers were successful. Mostly the guards put up a stout defence and there were often in-

stances of the mail-bags arriving safe but soaked with the blood of the gallant fellow who had suffered wounds or had died in their safe-keeping.

Many of the innkeepers along the great highways were in league with the highwaymen. It was a most unwise thing for a traveller to make show of much money at an inn. A crooked landlord would alert the robber of a likely victim and after the crime would share in the plunder. One of the reasons for the decline of highwaymen was the refusal by the authorities to license inns known to harbour outlaws. Another reason was that the roads were greatly improved towards the end of the eighteenth century. Capable engineers took the highways in hand and funds were raised for their upkeep and repair; these funds were largely supplied by the tolls paid at turnpikes, gates set at intervals along the main roads, where vehicles and riders had to pay a small fee before being allowed to pass. Travel was faster and safer.

However, the chief factor that eventually brought an end to the age of highwaymen was the establishment, particularly in the neighbourhood of London, of a regular, well-armed and uniformed Horse Patrol in 1805, and the

[31]

founding of the Metropolitan Police in 1829. But the rot had set into the highwayman's boots sometime before then, with the success of the original horse patrols instigated by the dedicated Fielding brothers, John and Henry, the Bow Street magistrates.

Highwaymen, in the traditional manner, persisted longer in the provinces. In 1807 the roads between Arundel and Chichester were the hunting grounds of a mounted robber named Allen, who preyed mostly on farmers returning home with full purses from market. The militia were called out to capture him and he was shot dead near Midhurst. Probably the last major case of highway robbery was reported in the *Illustrated London News* of 2 February 1850 and because of its interesting content it is worthy of quoting in full;

'CAPTURE OF HIGHWAYMEN – For some time past the neighbourhood of Bristol has been infested by a notorious gang of highwaymen known to the police under the appellation of the "Hanham and Cock-road Gang". To

[32]

HENRY FIELDING, NOVELIST AND MAGISTRATE.

such an extent have their depredations been carried, more
especially in the rural districts of Brislington and Keynsham, that many of the farmers are unwilling to attend, as
usual, our corn and other markets, several outrages have
been recently committed, attended with a great degree of
personal violence.

'A Mr Thomas White, a farmer of Balcombe, was
attacked the other day within a few hundred yards of a
farmhouse on the Frome Road by two armed men, who
demanded his money or his life; they dragged him off his
horse and commenced rifling his pockets. He shouted for
assistance, upon which they stuffed his mouth full of dirt
and robbed him of all his loose cash; his notes, which he
had placed in a private pocket, fortunately escaping their
notice. Mr Joseph Wyatt, farmer, of Wick, was attacked in
a similar manner near Lansdowne and robbed of his watch
and all that he had about him; the highwaymen also cut his
bridle reins and stirrups to prevent him pursuing them.

'Mr Wilkins of the Bell Inn, Chelwood, Somerset, was

[33]

waylaid by five men at the bottom of Knowle Hill, who robbed him and then made off in the direction of Keynsham. About an hour later the same evening, Mr Barrow, a blacksmith and farrier, who carries on business at Keynsham, was stopped; and although he resisted till he was nearly throttled, the blood gushing from his mouth and nostrils, he was robbed of five pounds. By the exertions of police-sergeant Hazell, five of the gang, named Samuel Bryant, William Powell, William Gunning, Samuel Rogers and John Rogers have been apprehended. One of them has turned approver [Queen's evidence], and some bludgeons have been found by the police at a spot indicated by him.

'The prisoners were examined on Saturday last and remanded, and it is stated that a great number of cases will be brought home to them. Subsequent to their apprehension another man, named Joseph Brittan, was taken into custody, and also the keeper of a beer-shop in the vicinity of Hanham, named Eli Tremlett, at whose house, the police received information, the gang used to meet. Great satisfaction was expressed by a host of farmers, who were present at the examination, at the capture of these desperate villains.'

As the highwaymen faded into history in England, similar types of mounted robbers developed in far-off Australia and the Wild West of the United States. The 'bushrangers' of Australia and the 'road agents' of America take the highwayman story to the turn of the twentieth century and these outlaws are dealt with in separate chapters.

[34]

CHAPTER TWO

The Gallows and the Gibbet

THE AGE OF THE HIGHWAYMAN was also the age of hanging. By 1800 hanging was the punishment for almost
every crime. Between 1749 and 1771 more than 250 highwaymen were executed at London's Tyburn gallows, not to
mention hundreds of other poor souls, men, women, and
children (the age of criminal responsibility being seven).
Indeed, it seems that the chief desire of the authorities was
to get rid of the 'criminal' classes by hanging or transporting
them.

The Parliamentary reward system, introduced in 1693,
offered £40 to anyone who could secure the conviction of a
highway robber. Having been captured and condemned to
death a highwayman – especially a celebrated one – was
expected to die bravely, nay, with panache, by the gloating
mob that gathered to witness his public execution. Charles
G. Harper in *Half-Hours with the Highwaymen* (1908) tells
us that;

'The hardened wretches who looked on at these last
scenes, and who had, many of them, already qualified for a
place in the [execution] cart, had a kind of perverted professional pride. They applauded when a malefactor, with
a curse and a jest, "died game", and they howled dis-
approval when some poor creatures broke down pitifully
on the verge of eternity.'

The star 'knights of the road' seldom disappointed their
audience. They dressed in their finest clothes for the last
ride to the gallows, waved and bowed to the crowded by-
standers on the journey, and generally behaved in a carefree
manner. Usually they delivered a speech, sometimes defiant,

sometimes penitent, before being 'turned off' by the hangman. Some performed a little dance on the gallows, others quipped to the last. Gallows humour, in particular the ironic, was greatly appreciated by the mob. One such gem has the highwayman rebuking the hangman for setting the noose too tight about his neck, saying, 'Hold, you rascal, have you a mind to strangle me?'

The day of his hanging was a day of glory for the well-known highwayman and he hogged the spotlight. There is a story of a dispute between a humble chimney-sweep and a celebrated highwayman who found themselves sharing the same cart on the road to Tyburn. As the elegant road-robber acknowledged his 'public' with extravagant gestures, the doomed sweep decided to get in on the act. 'Stand off, fellow!' exclaimed the star of the show, 'Do not steal my thunder.' To which the sweep replied, 'Stand off yourself, Mr Highwayman. I have as much right to be here as you.'

In London during the eighteenth century, Newgate was the highwayman's prison and Tyburn his place of execution,

[36]

Proverbs Chap: I. Vers: 27, 28.
When fear cometh as desolation, and their
destruction cometh as a Whirlwind; when
distress cometh upon them, then they shall
call upon God, but he will not answer.

Plate II

The Idle Apprentice executed at Tyburn engraved by William Hogarth, captures the pandemonium of a public hanging in the eighteenth century, an occasion known as 'Tyburn Fair'.

situated approximately where Marble Arch now stands. The gallows there was known as the 'triple tree' and the 'three-legged mare', being a triangular structure of three uprights topped by crossbeams, with accommodation for eight malefactors at a time on each side of the triangle – twenty-four hangings at one go! A Bow-street runner, early in the nineteenth century, recalled that in his youth he had often seen twelve, sixteen, or twenty persons hanged at a time and on two occasions forty hanged at a single session. Some gallows had a ladder which the condemned man would climb to be launched into eternity; Dick Turpin was hanged in this manner at York, throwing himself off the ladder.

Execution day at Tyburn was known as 'Tyburn Fair', a sporting occasion for which all London seemed to turn out.

[37]

[38]

Grand stands and scaffolding with seats were provided for those who could pay for the exhibition. Windows and roofs of neighbouring houses were packed. Hogarth recorded the awful scene in his series of engravings *The Idle Apprentice*. In 1727 Dean Swift wrote a savage satire, *Going to be Hanged*, concerning a highwayman's last ride to Tyburn;

As clever Tom Clinch, while the rabble was bawling,
Rode stately through Holborn to die at his calling,
He stopt at the 'Bowl' for a bottle of sack,
And promised to pay for it when he came back.
His waistcoat and stockings and breeches were white,
His cap had a new cherry ribbon to tie't.
The maids to the doors and the balconies ran,
And said, 'Lack-a-day, he's a proper young man!'
And as at the windows the ladies he spied,
Like a beau in the box, he bowed low on each side,
And when his last speech the loud hawkers did cry,
He swore from the cart, 'It was all a damn'd lie!'
The hangman for pardon fell down on his knee,
Tom gave him a kick in the guts for his fee,
Then said, 'I must speak to the people a little,
But I'll see you all damned before I will whittle!
My honest friend Wild (may he long hold his place),
He lengthen'd my life with a whole year of grace.
Take courage, dear comrades, and be not afraid,
Nor slip this occasion to follow my trade.
My conscience is clear, and my spirits are calm,
And thus I go off, without prayer-book or psalm.
Then follow the practice of clever Tom Clinch,
Who hung like a hero, and never would flinch.'

The journey in the condemned cart from Newgate to Tyburn was about three miles. The method of hanging was described by an eyewitness, a French Huguenot refugee, in the *Memoirs of Francois Misson* published in 1718;

'They put five or six in a cart (some gentlemen obtain leave to perform this journey in a coach) and carry them riding backwards, with a rope about their necks, to the fatal tree. The executioner stops the cart under one of the cross-beams and fastens to that ill-favoured beam one end of the rope, while the other is round the wrethe's [sic] neck. This done, he gives the horse a lash with his whip, away goes the cart, and there swings my gentleman kicking the air. The hangman does not give himself the trouble to put them out of their pain; but some of their friends or relations do it for them. They pull the dying person by the legs, and beat his breast to despatch him as soon as possible.'

The last person to be executed at Tyburn was John Austin, hanged there on 7 November 1783. Thereafter hangings in London took place on a gallows erected outside Newgate Prison. The last public hanging at Newgate was in 1868.

Executed highwaymen, especially the most notorious or those who had committed murder, also suffered the additional indignity of the gibbet – gibbeting being the hanging in chains of the dead bodies of criminals near the site where their crimes were committed, with the intention of serving as a warning to other highway robbers and to deter potential highwaymen. However, the dreadful gibbet was not successful in either case.

Throughout the eighteenth century and early into the nineteenth century gibbets were a common sight throughout the United Kingdom. They startled respectable travellers and their horses and attracted morbid sightseers. 'The chains rattled, the iron plates scarcely kept the gibbet together', wrote an eyewitness, 'and the rags of the highwaymen displayed their horrible skeletons.'

Relatives and friends of gibbeted highwaymen often stole the suspended bodies in order to give them a decent burial. In an article on gibbeting in *The Antiquary* of November 1890, the Rev. J. Charles Fox informed his readers that;

'It was usual to saturate the body with tar before it was hung in chains, in order that it might last the longer. This was done with the bodies of three highwaymen about the middle of the last century, gibbeted on the top of the Chevin, [a hill] near Belper, in Derbyshire. They had

[40]

The bodies of many executed highway robbers were hung on a gibbet at the roadside as a warning to other thieves. This practice was continued throughout the eighteenth century.

London's Newgate Prison, where Old Bailey now stands, was the final, grim abode of many highwaymen.

robbed the North Coach when it was changing horses at
the inn at Hazelwood, just below the summit of the Chevin.

'After the bodies had been hanging there a few weeks, one
of the friends of the criminals set fire, at night, to the big
gibbet that bore all three. The father of our aged informant,
and two or three others of the cottagers nearby, seeing a
glare of light, went up the hill, and there they saw the
sickening spectacle of the three bodies blazing away in the

A public hanging outside Newgate. The last public execution here took place in 1868.

darkness. So thoroughly did the tar aid this cremation that the next morning only the links of the iron chains remained on the site of the gibbet.'

Mail robbers were also candidates for the gibbet. *The Salisbury Journal* of 25 August 1783 records; 'On Tuesday morning William Weare was executed at Fisherton gallows for robbing the mail near Chippenham. The remaining part of the sentence was completed on Wednesday, by hanging the body in chains in Green Lane, near Chippenham, where it is now – as a dreadful momento to youth, how they swerve from the path of rectitude, and transgress the laws of their country.'

[43]

Sometimes (how often is not known) convicted murderers were barbarously hanged alive in chains. William Andrews in *Old Time Punishments* (1890) tells of a particular case;

'John Whitfield, a notorious highwayman, was gibbeted alive on Barrock, a hill a few miles from Wetherell, near Carlisle, about the year 1777. He lived at Coathill, and was the terror to all that part of the country, so that many would not venture out after nightfall, especially along the road by Barrock. It appears that he shot [and killed] a horseman in the open day, who was travelling to Armathwaite . . . It is said that he [Whitfield] hung [in chains] for several days, till his cries were heartrending, and a mail-coachman who was passing that way, put him out of his misery by shooting him.'

Although a patent failure as a deterrent, the grisly gibbet continued to disgrace the highways of England until the custom was abolished in 1834. The last man to be gibbeted in this country was George Cook, a murderer, whose body was suspended in chains in August 1832 at a spot near Leicester.

CHAPTER THREE

Crooked Cavaliers

IN THE AFTERMATH of the Civil War (1642-1649) between the supporters of King Charles I and Parliament, England swarmed with highwaymen. Many were Royalist ex-soldiers who turned to highway robbery in desperation. A goodly number were impoverished cavaliers, officers and gentlemen dispossessed of their estates and property by the victorious Parliament. They saw fit to play out the inter-regnum as 'knights of the road', stealing only, of course, from those crass supporters of the Commonwealth.

Here then, is the genesis of the gentleman highwayman, a cavalier well-mounted, dressed *a la mode*, booted and spurred, armed with a brace of pistols, and possessed of fine speech and courteous manner. Many were genuine ex-officers and born gentlemen, others of humble origin adopted a gentleman's style, all were mostly dubbed 'captain', even if they lacked just claim to that rank.

Typical of the cavalier crook was Captain Phillip Stafford, born about 1622, only son of a gentleman farmer of New-bury. For serving in the king's forces he was punished by the State by having his property sequestrated. Left penni-less, he took to the road to rob the society that had robbed him. He soon became a notorious highwayman, and was not particular who he preyed upon.

His depredations were brought to an end after he had robbed a farmer of £33 on the road to Reading. Con-demned to death, he went to his execution in a brave and carefree manner, thus establishing the proper gallows be-haviour of all true highwaymen who followed him. Stafford dressed for his death in his finest clothes, 'with a nosegay

[45]

Cavalier soldiers who fought for the king in the Civil War. Having lost the war, a number of Royalist officers became highwaymen and preyed on Roundhead travellers.

in his bosom', giving the appearance of a bridegroom rather than a condemned man. On the way to the gallows he had a final drink at a tavern, and laughingly promised to pay the landlord on his return journey.

Captain Zachary Howard was another of similar stamp. When civil war came he joined the king's banner, bringing with him a troop of horse he had raised himself by mortgaging his estate in Glamorganshire. With the war over and his king executed by the victors, Captain Howard set out to plague the regicides in the role of highwayman. But unlike Stafford, he was most particular who he robbed and humiliated.

A bold raider, he held up single-handed several top ranking Parliamentarians, even though they had escorts. When one of his victims reproved him for his recklessness, saying, 'Have you taken leave of your senses, sir, daring to venture against three armed men?' Howard replied, 'I would venture against ten men, with your idol Cromwell at the head.' And, we are told, he did indeed hold up Cromwell himself, but more of that later.

[46]

General Thomas Fairfax was next on Howard's list. In the civil war Fairfax had commanded the New Model Army and routed the king's forces at Naseby. On learning that Fairfax was sending a consignment of plate to his wife, Howard waylaid the transport and took the plate, also a letter to Lady Fairfax. Posing as a messenger, the highwayman delivered the letter and was invited to stay the night (General Fairfax being absent). With the household asleep, Howard arose, tied up and gagged all the servants, then raped Lady Fairfax and her daughter, riding off with a

[47]

sackful of plunder. The furious General Fairfax immediately offered £500 reward for the ravisher/robber.

Whether it is true or not that Howard did in fact beard Oliver Cromwell is open to argument. But here is the story. Both were staying at the same inn in Chester, and Howard ingratiated himself with the great man. The pious Cromwell invited the cunning cavalier to join him in prayers in his room; there, Captain Howard pointed a pistol at Cromwell's head and revealed his true identity. Having bound and gagged his eminent victim, the highwayman looted his possessions and, as a final humiliation, 'crowned' the Protector of England with a well-filled chamberpot! Such is the stuff of legends.

However, Howard's recklessness proved his undoing. One night on Blackheath he chanced his arm once too often in attempting to hold up six Roundhead officers single-handed. After a fierce fight he was overpowered and taken to Maidstone Gaol. It is said that Cromwell visited him there. Captain Zachary Howard was hanged in 1652.

In the same year that Howard danced on air, Captain James Hind, a much celebrated highwayman, also met his end on the gallows. Like Howard, he was an ardent royalist

[48]

Press card for a special showing
of the film, 'Ned Kelly'.

Publicity material for the film
'Ned Kelly' (1970).

Bushrangers of Australia holding
up a stage-coach.

The true Por
traiture of Captain
JAMES HIND
the Robber, who
died for Treafon.

who had distinguished himself in the civil war. But Hind
was not of gentle birth, being the son of a saddler of
Chipping Norton in Oxfordshire. He received a fair
education and was placed as apprentice to a butcher. A
clever, quick-learning lad, he improved his education,
manners and speech so that by the time he was notorious as
the 'grand thief' of England, he was as polished as any
gentleman.

By all accounts he was most polite and considerate to his
victims, except when he came across arrogant regicides like
Sergeant Bradshaw, the President of the Commission which
had sentenced Charles I to death. When Hind held up his

[49]

coach near Shaftesbury and ordered him to stand and deliver, the blustering Bradshaw endeavoured to intimidate the highwayman.

'Dost thou not know me, sir?' he demanded angrily, expecting the robber to put up his pistol and ride off in terror. 'I fear neither you nor any king-killing son of a whore', replied Hind, ending a lengthy condemnation with, 'Though I spare thy life as a regicide, be assured, that unless thou deliverest thy money immediately, thou shalt die for thy obstinacy.'

Bradshaw, suitably impressed, handed over his money without further ado. Hind also attempted to hold up the bigshot himself, Oliver Cromwell. Working with Thomas Allen and his gang, Hind ambushed Cromwell's coach on the road from Huntingdon to London. A strong escort guarded the coach and, after a short struggle, the raiders were chased off and Allen was among those captured. Hind escaped by riding his horse into the ground. Soon, his name was known all over the country. Here is an item published in a newspaper of September 1649;

'Last night was brought into this gaol [Bedford] two prisoners taken upon pursuit by the county, for robbing some soldiers of about £300 upon the highway, in the day-time; there were five in the fact, and are very handsome gentlemen; they will not confess their names, and therefore are supposed to be gentlemen of quality, and 'tis conceived they are of the knot of Captain Hind, that grand thief of England, that hath his associates upon the roads. They strewed at least £100 upon the way, to keep the pursuers doing [picking up the money], that they might not follow them.'

Hind had a touch of Robin Hood about him, he was known to help the poor and oppressed on occasion. One story tells of him riding through Warwick where he came upon an innkeeper being arrested for being unable to repay a £20 debt to the local money-lender. Hind settled the account himself, the sum was paid and the innkeeper re-leased. Later, the highwayman waylaid the usurer and recovered the £20, plus a large interest!

Another time, being hard-pressed for funds, he chanced upon an old man going to market to buy a cow so that his ten children should have milk. The old man had forty shillings on him, a paltry amount (to a man like Hind) that had taken the poor soul two years to save. Feeling great sympathy for the old man, Hind nevertheless needed the money, little though it was.

'My name is Hind, and if you will give me your forty shillings quietly, and meet me again this day week at this place, I promise to repay you double the sum. Only be cautious not to mention a word of this to anyone.' Hind was as good as his word. On the appointed day, having robbed a rich victim, he met the trusting old man again and handed over eighty shillings.

When Charles II attempted to regain the throne of England, loyal cavalier Captain Hind joined the king's forces and served in the battle of Worcester on 3 September 1651. The royalists were defeated and Hind escaped to London, where he lived under the name of James Brown. He was arrested in November 1651 and stood trial – not for highway robbery, but for treason, having fought for the king against Parliament. Found guilty, he was hanged, drawn and quartered as a traitor on 24 September 1652.

John Cottington, known as 'Mulled Sack', was another cavalier highwayman of humble origin. The youngest of nineteen children born to an alcoholic haberdasher of Cheapside, who drank himself into an early grave, John came into a harsh world in 1611. Apprenticed to a chimney-sweep at the age of eight, he ran away from that dirty trade five years later and became a pickpocket, at which he was most successful. He inherited his father's taste for wine, especially for good, warm sherry, hence his sobriquet 'Mulled Sack'.

He fought on the king's side in the Civil War, and thereafter returned to the lucrative game of picking pockets, but now, only those of the self-righteous Roundheads, or so he maintained. One of his prize victims was Lady Fairfax,

[51]

the same unfortunate woman whom Captain Howard robbed and raped.

Lady Fairfax arrived in her coach to attend a service at St Martin's Church, Ludgate. Suddenly the vehicle lurched sideways and threatened to turn over. Cottington, in elegant dress, was the first gentleman to come to the lady's assistance; which is not surprising since he had planned the removal of the axle pin that caused the coach to collapse. As he offered his hand to help, he deftly snipped her watch chain with a pair of scissors and pocketed a magnificent gold watch encrusted with diamonds.

Mulled Sack gave up picking pockets and became a highwayman; he teamed with Tom Cheney and they sought their victims on Hounslow Heath. On one occasion they held up Colonel Hewson, a Parliamentary officer, who was

John Cottington, known as 'Mulled Sack', offers Lady Fairfax his assistance, then steals her be-jewelled gold watch, seen hanging by a chain from her belt.

[52]

Cottington robs the army pay
wagon on Shotover Hill.

riding some distance ahead of his regiment. They took the
colonel's purse and galloped off with the soldiers in hot
pursuit. Cottington got away but Cheney was wounded and
captured and later hanged. Mulled Sack took up with a new
companion, Captain Horne, but he was also caught and
executed. From then on Cottington preferred to work alone.

His most daring and successful exploit was robbing the
army pay wagon carrying £4,000 for the garrison at
Gloucester. He stopped the wagon, which had an armed
escort, on Shotover Hill. He covered the soldiers with his
pistols before they realized what was happening. Before
riding off with his considerable loot, he delivered the
following rationale;

'This that I have taken, is as much mine as theirs who
own it, being all extorted from the public by the rapacious

[53]

Members of the Commonwealth to enrich themselves, maintain their janizaries [mercenary soldiers], and keep honest people in subjection.'

Like most of his calling, John Cottington ended up on the gallows. But he enjoyed a long run, being executed at the age of forty-five in 1656.

CHAPTER FOUR

Claude Duval

OF ALL THE STYLISH 'gentlemen of the road' it would seem that Claude Duval (or Du Vall) was the most dashing, the most charming, especially to the ladies, victims and paramours alike. Charles G. Harper, that serious though simple historian of highwaymen, has described the fancy Frenchman as one 'who ranks among his brother highwaymen as high as Rembrandt or Raphael among artists. He was, indeed, no less an artist in his own profession than they'. Duval has also been called 'an eternal feather in the cap of highway gentility'.

The truth about this Gallic gallant is difficult, if not impossible to determine. All the stories and anecdotes about him seem to spring from a single source, the *Memoirs of Monsieur Du Vall*, a biography penned by Dr William Pope, a professor of astronomy at Oxford and a member of the Royal Society, published in 1670, shortly after Duval's execution.

The *Memoirs* could well be called a chapbook of the superior kind. Patrick Pringle, in *Stand and Deliver* (1951), views it as a brilliant satire, poking sly fun – in Pope's own words – at 'the too great fondness of English ladies towards French footmen [a reference to Duval's earlier position]; which at that time of the day was too common a complaint'.

Pringle suggests that Pope's satire is so clever, so subtle that all subsequent historians and writers have missed the doctor's point and swallowed Duval's supposed adventures hook, line and sinker. Which indeed seems to be the case. The situation, however, is understandable for there is very little other contemporary material. With this in mind let me relate the traditional story of Claude Duval, a version based on Pope and embellished by numerous writers over the last 300 years.

According to Pope, Duval was born at Domfront, Normandy in 1643. He was not a gentleman born, as was generally believed, but the offspring of a humble miller and a tailor's daughter. At about fourteen years old, Claude left home and went to seek his fortune in Rouen, the capital of Normandy, and there was hired by a party of exiled English royalists to look after their horses on the journey to Paris.

When Charles II was restored to the English throne in 1660, Claude came to England as the footman of an English noble, in whose household he picked up his good English and fine manners. It is not known exactly when he turned to highway robbery. In 1666 a newsletter mentioned him by name in the following report;

'Last Monday week in Holborn Fields, while several gentlemen were travelling to Newmarket, to the races there, a Highwayman very politely begged their purses, for he said he was advised that he should win a great sum if he adventured some guineas with the competers at Newmarket on a certain horse called "Boopeepe" [Bo-peep], which my Lord Excetter [Exeter] was to run a match. He was so pressing that they resigned their money to his keeping (not without sight of his pistols); he telling them that, if they would give him their names and the names of the places where they might be found, he would return to them that [they] had lent, at usary [with interest]. It is thought that his venture was not favourable, for the gentlemen have not received neither principle or interest. It is thought that it was Monsieur Claud Du Vall, or one of his knot, that ventured the gentlemen's money for them.'

By 1668 Duval headed a list of highwaymen in a Royal Proclamation that offered £20 for his capture. Apparently, he was a true knight of the road, fashionably dressed and courteous in manner and speech, to which he added a Gallic flourish much appreciated by the ladies. Duval greatly loved the ladies, and they were quick to respond. His amorous conquests were said to be large in number and included all kinds of women – serving girls, widows and wives, whores, and ladies of wealth and rank.

Full of *joie de vivre* he was an enthusiastic dancer and his most celebrated exploit concerns his alfresco dance on Hounslow Heath. Dr Pope originated the episode, so let him tell it;

'He with his squadron overtakes a coach, which they had set overnight, having intelligence of a booty of £400 in it. In the coach was a knight, his lady, and only one serving-maid, who perceiving five horsemen making up to them, presently imagined that they were beset . . . The Lady, to show that she was not afraid, takes a flageolet [a kind of flute] out of her pocket and plays. Du Vall takes the hint, plays also, and excellently well, upon a flageolet of his own, and in this posture he rides up to the coach-side.

' "Sir," says he to the person in the coach, "your lady plays excellently, and I doubt not but she dances as well. Will you please to walk out of the coach and let me have the honour to dance one currant [coranto] with her upon the heath?" "Sir," said the person in the coach, "I dare not

The dashing Duval and his gang
hold up a coach.

deny anything to one of your quality and good mind. You
seem a gentleman, and your request is very reasonable.''

'Which said, the lacquey opens the door, out comes the
knight, Du Vall leaps lightly off his horse and hands the
lady out of the coach. They danced, and here it was that
Du Vall performed marvels; the best masters in London,
except those that are French, not being able to show such
footing as he did in his great French riding boots. The
dancing being over, he waits on the lady to her coach. As
the knight was going in, says Du Vall to him, ''Sir, you
have forgot to pay the musick.'' ''No, I have not,'' replies
the knight, and putting his hand under the seat of the coach,
pulls out a hundred pounds in a bag, and delivers it to

Claude Duval dancing a coranto
on Hounslow Heath, from the
painting by W. P. Frith, R.A.

[58]

him, which Du Vall took with a very good grace and courteously answered, "Sir, you are liberal, and shall have no cause to repent your being so. This liberality of yours shall excuse you the other three hundred pounds." '

So the coach rattled on its journey, with all involved pleased with the happening. Duval being satisfied with his haul, the knight thankful for getting off so lightly, and the lady enchanted with the dancing highwayman, a tale she would relate with relish to her female friends. There is only one anecdote in Dr Pope's *Memoirs* that shows Duval in a mean mood, and it is this.

On Blackheath, Duval and his gang held up a coach full of ladies, one of them was feeding a baby from a silver sucking bottle. Having relieved the ladies of their money and valuables, Duval snatched the silver feeding bottle from the baby's mouth. He would have kept it had not one of his colleagues persuaded him to give it back, reminding the Frenchman that he enjoyed the reputation of a gentleman robber and such an ignoble act would harm his standing. Over the centuries other writers have changed Pope's story somewhat; it is another of the gang who takes the baby's silver bottle, and the gallant Duval who orders him to give it back!

Another episode tells of Duval riding in Windsor Forest where he encountered Roper, the master of buckhounds to Charles II, and commanded that stout huntsman to stand and deliver at gunpoint. Roper did so without hesitation and the highwayman galloped off, fifty guineas the richer. Dr Pope and other writers have credited Duval with every kind of criminal attribute. He was a considerable confidence trickster and once, posing as an alchemist, diddled a greedy priest out of a large sum of money by performing a scientific trick involving a 'philosophical powder' that appeared to turn base metals into gold. He was an expert card-sharper with a playing manner 'so pleasant, so apparently honest that he was never suspected'. A calculating gambler with a mathematical mind, he would wager on

[60]

Duval runs into Roper, the king's
master of buckhounds, and
relieves him of fifty guineas at
gunpoint.

virtually anything – the length of a stick, the distance of a
certain object – and always win.

Like others of his kind, when in funds, Duval indulged
himself hugely in wine, women, and song. And it was a
surfeit of strong drink which proved his undoing. A large
reward was continually offered for him. At last he was
taken, blind drunk in the Hole-in-the-Wall tavern in
Chandos Street, at the back of London's Strand. Fortunate
it was for the bailiff and his men that our hero was drunk
and incapable, otherwise, in the words of Dr Pope . . . 'they
would have tasted his prowess; for he had in his pocket
three pistols, one whereof could shoot twice, and by
his side an excellent sword which, managed by such a hand
and heart, must without doubt, have done wonders . . . I
have heard it attested by those that knew how good a marks-
man he was, and his excellent way of fencing, that had he
been sober, it was impossible he could have killed less than
ten.'

Committed to Newgate, Duval was tried, convicted, and
sentenced to death. While in prison, the handsome Frenchman was visited by many women of rank. Some of them
attempted to secure a pardon for him, and failing in this,
they accompanied him to the gallows at Tyburn, their faces
masked. He was executed on 21 January 1670, aged twenty-
seven years. He faced his end bravely. His body was taken
by friends to the Tangier Tavern in St Giles, where it lay
in state, watched over by a bodyguard. He was given a fine
funeral in St Paul's Church, Covent Garden, his grave-
stone inscribed with the fitting epitaph;

> Here lies Du Vall. Reader, if male thou art,
> Look to they purse. If female, to thy heart.
> Much havoc has he made of both, for all
> Men he made stand, and women he made fall.
> The second Conqueror of the Norman race,
> Knights to his arm did yield, and ladies to his face.
> Old Tyburn's glory, England's illustrious thief,
> Du Vall, the ladies' joy, Du Vall, the ladies' grief.

So passed Claude Duval, the romantic rogue, but let Dr Pope, master of irony, have the last word. He claimed that Duval left behind a 'dying confession' that he had intended to read at Tyburn, but did not. In this mysterious document Duval thanks his highborn female admirers for trying to secure him a pardon, ending with his sting in the tail;

'Nevertheless, ladies, it does not grieve me that your intercession for my life proved ineffectual. Had you saved my life I would, in gratitude, have devoted it wholly to you, which yet would have been too short; for had you been sound, I should have soon died of consumption, if otherwise, of the pox.'

CHAPTER FIVE

Gentlemen of the Road

HIGHWAY ROBBERY was often the final recourse for hitherto
'respectable' gentlemen who found themselves without
money or support, having wasted their inherited wealth in
gambling and dissolute living. The criminal records of the
eighteenth century contain many cases of young rakes of
good birth who became highwaymen, and mostly died on
the gallows. Two prime examples are William Parsons, an
Old Etonian, and James Maclaine, known as the 'Gentleman
Highwayman'.

The short, sinful life of William Parsons, Esquire, as he
is honoured in all contemporary accounts, is a classic tale
of a Rake's Progress. Born in 1717, he was the youngest
son of a baronet of the county of Nottingham and a nephew
of the Duchess of Northumberland. At fourteen he was
sent to Eton where he soon gained notoriety for his petty
thefts from his schoolfellows and for his growing passion
for the gaming table.

He was punished for his stealing with a brutal flogging
during which 'the skin was flayed off his back and afterwards rubbed with pickle; yet not all the punishments he
suffered, though ever so severe, could eradicate his natural
propensity for wickedness'.

Removed from Eton, he was sent to live with an uncle,
Captain Dutton, at Epsom. Again his profligacy ruined the
relationship and he was thrown out. Another relative took
on the task of trying to inculcate William with a respect
for other people's property, but to no avail. After playing
'several slippery tricks', William was sent to sea by his
exasperated family, the navy being 'the general resource
for such sorts of sparks'.

[63]

He sailed as a midshipman on H.M.S. *Drake* to the West Indies; caught cheating at cards he had to leave the navy. Owing to this disgrace and other blackguard deeds his aunt, the Duchess of Northumberland, excluded William from her will. Back in England he cast around for a convenient source of income. Of pleasing figure, with an easy and polite manner of address, he found little difficulty in marrying, in 1740, a young lady with a considerable fortune.

He soon dissipated his dowry of £4,000 at the gaming tables and entered the army as an ensign. His continuing bad conduct forced him to leave the service and he became heavily in debt. Having landed in gaol on a charge of forgery, he was sentenced to seven years transportation to the American colonies, there to work as a slave in the plantations of Virginia.

Seven weeks after arriving in America, Parsons came to the notice of Lord Fairfax, who knew his family; Fairfax obtained his freedom, took him into his house and treated

Dick Turpin clearing the old
  Hornsey toll bar gate.

Jesse James and his gang hold
up a train.

William Parsons was addicted to gambling. The money he stole was quickly dissipated at the gambling tables. Illustration by Gillray, published in 1796.

him in a most kind and hospitable manner. The incorrigible Parsons repaid this kindness by stealing his benefactor's finest horse and committing highway robbery on the roads of Virginia. With the money thus gained he bought passage to England.

Here he continued his new profession of highwayman, plaguing the country between Turnham Green and Houns-low Heath. One night he stopped a postchaise on the heath and robbed two gentlemen of five guineas, some silver, and a watch. A short time later he held up a lone traveller at midnight near Turnham Green and took from him thirty shillings and a gold ring. Whereupon the victim asked for the return of the ring for sentimental reasons. Parsons gave it back, together with five shillings out of the thirty, and said; 'I can assure you, sir, that nothing but the most pressing necessity could have forced me to rob you.' The victim shook hands with the highwayman, saying, 'And I can assure you, sir, that owing to your gentlemanly behaviour, I shall not prosecute if I should hear of your being apprehended.'

[65]

Parsons was finally captured by two intended victims, who turned the tables on him. One Sunday morning on Hounslow Heath he came upon two gentlemen travelling in a postchaise; one of them suspected the lone rider to be a highwayman and ordered him to keep his distance. Parsons held back, not knowing if the men were armed, but he followed the carriage towards Hounslow town, hoping to take them at a disadvantage.

Foolishly he rode behind the carriage into the town, whereupon the two men alighted and demanded his sur-render, saying they would alarm the townsfolk if he did not comply immediately. Thinking he could bluff his gentle-manly way out of trouble, Parsons gave up his pistols and was taken to the Rose and Crown, where the landlord announced that Parsons answered the description of the highwayman who had long troubled the area.

It was the end of the road for William Parsons, Esquire. Committed to Newgate, he stood trial at the Old Bailey, was found guilty of returning from transportation, and for this was sentenced to death. Despite strong efforts by his family to obtain a reprieve, he was hanged at Tyburn on 11 February 1750.

James Maclaine (or Maclean) was a contemporary of William Parsons, and indeed both were hanged in the same year. Maclaine was known in his own lifetime as 'the Gentleman Highwayman'. Born in 1724 at Monaghan, in the north of Ireland, he was the youngest son of a Scots Presbyterian minister. The oldest son, Archibald, also took orders and became the pastor of the English congregation at The Hague. James was given a good education, was taught Latin, and became 'a perfect master of writing and accompts [accounts]', in preparation for a career as a merchant.

He was eighteen when his father died; the frugal minister leaving him enough money to set himself up in business. But James had no mind for the dull life of trading and figures. A free agent now with money to spend, he 'equipped himself in the gayest dress he could procure, bought a fine

[66]

gelding, and set up as a man of fashion'. He moved to Dublin and there, in bad company, he soon ran through his money. A sorry, sadder – but no wiser – man, he turned to his relatives for aid and was spurned.

After a short, unhappy period in service as a footman and a butler, Maclaine made his way to England, where he married the daughter of a London horse-dealer and inn-keeper. With his dowry of £500 he set up business as a grocer and chandler. But his trading ability was not as strong as his passion for pleasure, gambling, and his desire to appear as a gentleman. The business failed, his wife died, and he fell in with a bankrupt apothecary named Plunkett, a dubious character 'who had lived all his life on the sharp'.

It was Plunkett who suggested that they take to the road to recoup their 'lost fortunes'. Having procured pistols and horses and wearing 'Venetian masques', they waylaid some

[67]

graziers returning from Smithfield Market, and from one victim Plunkett took £70. Maclaine, however, had little heart for robbery. He was nervous in the extreme. He took no active part in the initial foray; overcome with fear he lost the power to speak or to draw his pistol. 'After the robbery he rode for miles without speaking; when they reached an inn he hid himself, and seemed afraid of his very shadow.'

Their next endeavour involved holding up the St Alban's coach and in this Maclaine again displayed a singular lack of fortitude. After stopping the coach on Hounslow Heath, he lost his nerve altogether and galloped off, leaving Plunkett to handle the situation as best he could. However, the reluctant highwayman gathered his wits and returned to find his partner still covering the travellers with his pistol, and helped him relieve their victims of money and valuables.

Despite his comrade's feeble behaviour, Plunkett stuck with him and they kept busy; during the next six months they committed some sixteen robberies, in Hyde Park, near Marylebone, and other spots within twenty miles of London. One night in 1749 they held up Horace Walpole, the noted author and Member of Parliament, in Hyde Park. During this episode Maclaine's nervousness nearly resulted in death; he accidentally discharged his pistol, the bullet, said Walpole, 'razed the skin under my eye, left some marks of shot on my face, and stunned me. The ball went through the top of the carriage and, if I had sat an inch nearer to the left side, must have gone through my head.' Maclaine was stricken with remorse and the next morning Walpole received a well-phrased letter of profuse apology from the robber. Walpole later recalled that 'the whole affair was conducted with the greatest good breeding on both sides'.

The Gentleman Highwayman, as he was now called, lived on his loot in high style. He had grand rooms in St James's Street, dressed in extravagant fashion, kept an expensive mistress, and was well-known in the gaming rooms and *salons* of London society. Witty and charming in conversation, he was extremely popular with the ladies.

[68]

He was perfectly suited to playing the role of a gentleman of private means, and when those means ran low he took to the road again, albeit reluctantly. However, his boldness improved with the more robberies he committed.

One June morning in 1750 he and Plunkett held up the Salisbury stage at Turnham Green; ordering the five male passengers to alight, they robbed them of all they had, but the one lady traveller they treated with courtesy and took only what she chose to offer. Later the same day, on Hounslow Heath, they came upon Lord Eglinton in a postchaise with two mounted servants. Eglinton was armed with a blunderbuss and presented it at the highwaymen. Maclaine, behaving with unusual courage, refused to be intimidated and levelled his pistol at the stubborn nobleman, demanding that he put down his weapon, which he did. The robbers made off with Eglinton's valuables, the blunderbuss, and a splendid coat embellished with gold lace.

Maclaine and Plunkett hold up the Earl of Eglinton on Hounslow Heath. Maclaine, at the rear, forces the Earl to put down his blunderbuss.

[70]

Maclaine in chains in the condemned cell at Newgate, where he was visited by many prominent people and lady admirers.

The 'remarkable coat' led to Maclaine's downfall. When he attempted to dispose of the loot to a pawnbroker, the coat was recognized from the description on a reward poster and Maclaine was arrested. Plunkett, more canny than his accomplice, vanished from the scene and was never caught.

Maclaine's trial at the Old Bailey was a social occasion, the courtroom crowded with prominent and fashionable people, mostly fine ladies who had known and entertained the accused. Lady Caroline Petersham, one of nine witnesses that Maclaine called to speak on his behalf, proclaimed; 'My Lords, I have had the pleasure to know him well. He has often been about my house and I never lost anything.'

Found guilty, Maclaine was sentenced to death. While in the condemned cell at Newgate, he was visited by three thousand curious people (according to Walpole), most of them society folk who displayed great sympathy for the Gentleman Highwayman. Deeply repentant of his deeds, the minister's wayward son turned to the Bible for solace. Hanged at Tyburn on 3 October 1750, he made no farewell speech to the mob, his last words being; 'May God forgive my enemies and receive my soul.'

Maclaine was a well-known frequenter of London's fashionable gaming rooms and was popular with society hostesses.

[71]

CHAPTER SIX

Jonathan Wild

NO HISTORY OF HIGHWAYMEN is complete without an account of Jonathan Wild, the self-proclaimed 'Thief-taker General of Great Britain and Ireland'. While appearing to uphold the law to the public at large, Wild was in fact the 'Regulator' of the London underworld, the commander-in-chief of the gangster legions that infested the metropolis. He organized and controlled virtually all criminal activity in and around the city.

If a villain flouted Wild's authority, the treacherous thief-taker would arrest him, collect the reward, and give evidence against the man that would send him to prison or the gallows. When Wild himself was brought to trial in 1725, he distributed among the jurymen a list of some 100 criminals he had brought to justice, including thirty-five highwaymen and the celebrated Jack Sheppard. However, this mitigative record of arrests did not save him from the hangman.

Wild was a super 'fence' who would restore stolen property (having instigated the theft himself) to its owner for a suitable reward, and no questions asked. His transactions with the unsuspecting victims were proper, polite, and cloaked with an impressive display of thorough book-keeping 'legality'. Wild had great audacity and style.

He was born in Wolverhampton in May 1683, his father being a joiner and his mother a marketwoman. Jonathan learned to read and write at the Free School. He was apprenticed to a buckle-maker in the town and married in 1701. Rejecting his humble, humdrum life, he deserted his wife and child and made his way to London, where he got

Jonathan Wild, the crooked
'Thief-taker General', arresting a
highwayman.

[73]

into debt and landed in the Wood Street Compter, a prison for debtors.

During his four years in the Compter he gained a thorough grounding in the criminal life of London. There he formed an intimate relationship with a prostitute named Mary Milliner (or Molyneux) and when they were both released in 1712 – by the newly passed Act of Parliament for the relief of debtors – they set up a small brothel in Lewkenor's Lane (now Macklin Street), Covent Garden. In this hell's kitchen of whores, thieves, and villains of every stripe Jonathan completed his education in criminality.

He soon became acquainted with the various robber gangs, their methods and haunts. He did not join them in their thieving operations for that was too risky; he was content for the time being to act as Mary's ponce, or pimp. He observed that the basic problem facing all thieves was not the acquisition of stolen property, but its disposal. And so he became a fence, a dealer in stolen goods.

He set up shop in Cripplegate and advertised his business. He invited victims of recent robberies to visit his office, where he would take note of the missing property, and then, through his extensive knowledge of the underworld he would endeavour to regain the goods and return them to the rightful owner. For this service Wild charged an initial consultation fee of five shillings and fifty per cent of the market value of the items returned. He split the 'reward' money fifty-fifty with the thieves. At that time no law existed for the punishment of receivers of stolen goods.

His bounding success as a fence earned him a growing influence in the underworld. His comprehensive knowledge of criminal activity placed many thieves in his power; he began to manipulate them, and if they dared disobey his commands he would turn them over to the law. A leading officer of the London law at that time was Charles Hitchen, the Under (or Second) City Marshal, a thoroughly corrupt man who had purchased the post in order to line his pockets. Among his various crooked enterprises, Hitchen ran a protection racket, extorting money from criminals and the

[74]

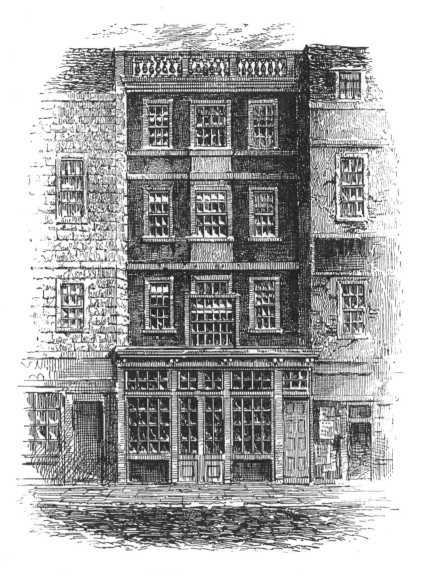

owners of certain establishments in return for not prosecuting them.

Wild gained Hitchen's confidence and in 1713 became the Marshal's 'Man', or assistant; Jonathan inflated his position by calling himself the 'Deputy Marshal of the City of London', a title to which he had no right. But it impressed the ignorant criminals and gullible victims with whom he dealt. Later, having brought to justice some sixty male-

[75]

factors, Wild proclaimed himself in the press 'Thief-taker General of Great Britain and Ireland'.

Although a physically small man, he was wiry and strong and not short on courage; indeed, during his ten years of active thief-taking he suffered two fractures of his skull and seventeen wounds from swords, daggers, and bullets in apprehending villains.

He arrested his first highwayman, James Goodman, in March 1716. Having robbed a traveller in Epping Forest, Goodman was caught and jailed but managed to escape. Wild was informed of his whereabouts and, in company with the turnkeys of Newgate, went to take the desperate highwayman. Goodman put up a stubborn fight but was eventually overpowered, and later hanged.

Another of Wild's exploits was reported in the *Weekly Journal* of 13 June 1719; 'Jonathan Wild, the British Thief-Taker, going down last week into Oxfordshire with a warrant from the Lord Chief Justice to apprehend two notorious highwaymen . . . met them within a few miles of Oxford on the road. But they hearing of his design met him, and one of them fired a pistol at him; but Jonathan . . . received no hurt, and then he discharged a pistol at them, which wounded one of them so terribly that his life is in great danger [he died later]; the other was pursued and taken and committed to Oxford Gaol, and Jonathan has given security to appear at the next Assizes to justify his conduct.'

Wild in his assumed position of 'Deputy Marshal of the City of London' now tightened his grip on the city's underworld, over which he desired total power. He organized the gangs and divided the metropolis and its environs into districts, each gang to operate only in its appointed district. He planned robberies and set his minions to carry them out. He forced the other fences out of business and obtained the monopoly in stolen goods. At the same time he maintained his public image of thief-taker and honest restorer of missing property. It was, however, a somewhat tarnished image and he was charged several times with receiving stolen goods, but was acquitted on each count.

In 1718 Parliament passed an Act intended to plug the hole in the existing law concerning the traffic in stolen goods. A particular clause, aimed specifically at Wild's nefarious operations, read as follows;

'And whereas there are divers persons who have secret acquaintance with felons, and who make it their business to help persons to their stolen goods, and by that means gain money from them, which is divided between them and the felons, whereby they greatly encourage such offenders. Be it enacted, by the authority aforesaid, that whenever any person taketh money or reward, directly or indirectly, under pretence, or upon account of helping any person or persons to any stolen goods or chattels, every such person so taking money or reward as aforesaid (unless such person do apprehend, or cause to be apprehended, such felon who stole the same, and give evidence against him) shall be guilty of felony, according to the nature of the felony committed in stealing such goods, and in such and the same manner as if such offender had stolen such goods and chattels, in the manner, and with such circumstances, as the same were stolen.'

This clause, framed in particular with Wild in mind, caused the Act to be called the 'Jonathan Wild Act'. But it failed to deter him, he simply went about his crooked business with more circumspection. In 1719 he moved to prestigious premises very near the Old Bailey, which gave his 'Lost Property Office' a lawful façade. He further embellished his appearance of authority by carrying a short silver staff topped with a crown.

When a client called at his office to retrieve missing goods, Wild no longer charged an initial (and illegal) fee. He would make much show of recording the particulars of the robbery, the description of the stolen items and their value (all of which he knew already). He would then ask the client to call again in a few days, by which time he would surely have good news concerning the goods in question. On the second, or third meeting Wild would advise the person to send a servant to a certain spot at a particular time and there a man (Wild's agent) would hand over the missing property – in direct exchange for a stated sum of money.

He was frequently asked how it was possible that he could carry on the business of restoring stolen goods and yet not be in league with the robbers, to which he would always reply;

'My acquaintance among thieves is very extensive, and when I receive information of a robbery, I make enquiry after the suspected parties, and leave word at proper places, that if the goods are left where I appoint, the reward shall be paid, and no questions asked. Surely no imputation of guilt can fall upon me; for I hold no interviews with the robbers, nor are the goods given into my possession.'

Wild believed in keeping his name in the public conscience. Here is a typical advertisement of his, one of hundreds, published in the *Daily Post* of 2 November 1724;

'Lost, the 1st October, a black shagreen pocket-book, edged with silver, with some notes of hand. The said book was lost in the Strand, near the Fountain Tavern, about 7 or 8 o'clock at night. If any person will bring the aforesaid book to Mr Jonathan Wild, in the Old Bailey, he shall have a guinea reward.'

Jonathan Wild prospered greatly. He was the undisputed king of crime. If a criminal displeased him he sold out the offender to the law for the £40 reward. One young man who did rebel against the tyrant was Jack Sheppard, a highwayman and housebreaker. When Jack and his mate Joseph 'Blueskin' Blake flouted Wild's authority and dealt independently with a small-time fence named William Field, the 'thief-taker general' induced Field to turn King's evidence against the 'renegades' and he arrested them both.

When Wild attended Blueskin's trial at the Old Bailey, the furious highwayman seized the double-dealer and slashed his throat; but the penknife was blunt and he did not succeed in killing Wild, he did, however, inflict a serious throat wound. Despite the fact that Wild was now

unable to give evidence against him, Blueskin Blake was
sentenced to death and went to the gallows saying he
would have died contented if he had finished off the
treacherous thief-taker. Jack Sheppard also perished at
Tyburn, but not before he had made several spectacular
escapes from prison; his exploits are dealt with in the next
chapter.

[79]

Wild recovered from Blueskin's attack, but his general health and vigour deteriorated. His bureau of exchange between victims and thieves was used less and less and he took to buying stolen goods direct from criminals and storing the stuff in secret warehouses, from where it was smuggled across the Channel to Holland in Wild's own boat. At last he was arrested, in February 1725, on a Warrant of Detainer that listed eleven charges against him, number one being, 'That for many years past he had been a confederate with great numbers of highwaymen, pick-pockets, house-breakers shop-lifters, and other thieves.'

He stood trial at the Old Bailey on 15 May 1725, charged specifically with instigating the theft of fifty yards of lace, receiving the stolen material and selling it back to the owner *without making any effort to bring the thief to justice*.

An invitation to Wild's execution, drawn by William Hogarth.

Doomed by the 'Jonathan Wild Act' of 1718, he was found guilty and sentenced to death. Wild, however, had decided to cheat the hangman and the mob that bawled for his blood.

On the morning of execution day he attempted to poison himself with a huge dose of laudanum, but it was not enough to kill him and he remained in a semi-conscious state to the end. As he rode the cart to Tyburn on 24 May 1725 the hostile crowds lining the streets threw stones and dirt at him, cursing and reviling him. The London under-world, and many a highwayman, breathed a sigh of relief at the passing of 'Judas' Wild.

Wild on his way to the Tyburn gallows. The hostile crowd cursed and threw stones and dirt at him.

Jack Sheppard in Newgate, old
engraving after the portrait by
Sir James Thornhill.

CHAPTER SEVEN

Jack Sheppard

JOHN SHEPPARD was a jack-of-all-thieving-trades; high-wayman, footpad, and housebreaker. He was undistin-guished in all three roles, yet he is ranked high among the most famous criminals of the eighteenth century. He earned his prominent position in the annals of crime by his most remarkable escapes from prison that made him the talk of the land, the subject of countless ballads, plays, books, portraits – and a sermon.

John, known as 'Jack' Sheppard was born in Spitalfields, London, in March 1702, the youngest son of a carpenter. Jack was apprenticed to a carpenter named, appropriately, Owen Wood. He soon manifested a crooked bent, stealing from the houses in which he carried out carpentry jobs. He kept bad company and formed a relationship with a girl pickpocket, Elizabeth Lyon, known to her criminal coterie as 'Edgeworth Bess'.

She was a big, beefy girl while Jack was small and slight, a proper cockney sparrow. However, he was wiry and sur-prisingly strong and his manikin physique served him well in his escapes from prison. Jack was about nineteen when he quit the carpentry trade for a full-time life of crime. He joined the gang of thieves which included his elder brother Tom. They robbed houses and shops and Jack's skills as carpenter and locksmith made him a valuable member of the gang, part of the Jonathan Wild organization.

When Tom Sheppard was caught in February 1724 (and was later transported to America) he was induced to put the finger on his young brother and Jack was incarcerated in the St Giles's Roundhouse, in an upper chamber two stories from the ground. He escaped on the first night. Using a broken razor and a piece of chain he broke through the roof and, tying together some blankets, lowered himself into the churchyard below and walked away. Jack was clever in escaping but not in retaining his freedom.

He was soon recaptured and committed to New Prison at Clerkenwell. When Edgeworth Bess came to visit him there, she too was arrested. Regarded as husband and wife, they were confined together in one room. Friends smuggled Jack some tools and he got to work. Early on the Whit-Monday morning of 25 May he had filed off his own fetters and removed an iron bar from the window. By means of a blanket he lowered the buxom Bess thirty-two feet to the ground; but first she had to divest herself of gown and petticoat to enable her to squeeze through the narrow window opening. Jack tossed her clothes after her and lowered himself to the prison yard. They were not yet free.

There still remained a wall twenty-two feet high to overcome. At the gate, the agile Jack climbed the protruding locks and bolts to the top of the wall. He helped Bess over and they were in the street and away. Jack was now a celebrity among his fellow crooks and considered himself something of a bigshot, big enough to defy the rigid control of Jonathan Wild, the master fence and thief-taker. Jack started to deal independently with a small-time fence named William Field, who offered better prices than Wild, and the latter decided to crush the young rebel.

Jack teamed up with Joseph Blake, a highwayman and footpad known as 'Blueskin', from his dark countenance. They committed a number of robberies together, several of them on Hampstead Heath, where they held up stagecoaches. They also broke into Mr Kneebone's drapery shop in the Strand and removed a large amount of cloth. Mr Kneebone sought the help of the influential Jonathan Wild, who seized the opportunity to put down Jack and Blueskin. He sent his trusted assistant Quilt Arnold to arrest Sheppard. As Arnold burst into his room, Jack clapped a pistol to the thief-taker's breast, but the weapon misfired and

Arnold dragged Jack off to New Prison. Blueskin was arrested later.

Brought before Mr Justice Blackerby, Jack saw fit to confess to three highway robberies and three cases of house-breaking. He was transferred to Newgate and appeared at the Old Bailey Sessions in August 1724. Jonathan Wild induced Field the fence to give evidence against Sheppard, who was found guilty and sentenced to death, the execution to take place on 4 September.

Jack, in the condemned cell, was visited by Bess and another girl. He had already managed to cut through one of the links of his fetters and freed his legs, and had partially sawn through an iron bar in the barrier at which visitors were allowed to speak to the condemned. With the two women wailing and lamenting loudly Jack's coming execution, thus covering the sound of his rasping file, Sheppard completed the cutting of the iron bar. Big Bess and her mate then pulled Jack's small, slim body through the gap, wrapped him in a large cloak and walked him to freedom.

Jack was at large for ten days; the time of his intended execution came and went. He was now the talk of London; to escape from the condemned cell at Newgate was a feat indeed. Sheppard joined forces with a butcher-boy named William Page, who idolized him, and they took to robbing on Finchley Common. When the keepers of Newgate learned of his whereabouts a strong posse of horsemen was sent to the common and soon nabbed Jack and his new companion.

Back in the condemned cell at Newgate, Sheppard was chained down to the floor with double irons. But his cheeky cockney humour, and his desire to escape, never diminished. London's high society beat a perfumed path to his smelly cell, anxious to meet the man of the moment, the man whom no prison could hold. He would entertain his admiring visitors with colourful tales of his criminal adventures and audacious escapes. His guests were sympathetic in word and deed, for he was a beguiling young villain, and they left him food, money, and *tools*. On several occasions

Jack's girlfriend, 'Edgeworth Bess', helps him escape from the condemned cell at Newgate. From a contemporary print.

the turnkeys found small files, a chisel and a hammer on his person and concealed about his cell.

Finally, it was considered necessary to remove him from the condemned cell to the strongest room in the prison, a place called the 'Castle', where he was heavily chained to the floor day and night. When Austin the turnkey discovered that the indomitable Jack had been tampering with his irons, he said; 'Young man, I see what you have been doing. I understand that it is your business to make good

[86]

Contemporary print illustrating
the many obstacles that Jack
overcame in his great escape from
the 'Castle' strong-room at Newgate.

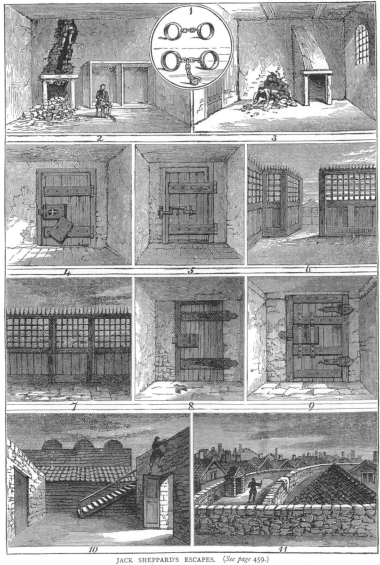

JACK SHEPPARD'S ESCAPES. *(See page* 459.)

1. Handcuffs and Feetlocks, and Padlock to Ground.   2. Cell over the Castle, Jack Sheppard fastened to the floor. Climbing up the
Chimney, where he found a bar of iron.   3. Red Room over the Castle, into which he got out of the Chimney.   4. Door of the
Red Room, the lock of which he put back.   5. Door of the Entry between the Red Room and the Chapel.   6. Door
going into the Chapel, which he burst open.   7. Door going out of the Chapel towards the Leads.   8. Door with a Spring Lock,
which he opened.   9. Door over the same Passage.   10. The Lower Leads.   11. The Higher Leads, the walls of which he
got over, and descended by the staircase off the roof of a turner's house into the street.

your escape, if you can, and it is mine to take care you shall
not.' To which Jack replied, 'Then let us both look to our
business.'

Jack did break out of the Castle. It was his greatest triumph over locks, walls and other obstacles. He chose the afternoon of 15 October 1724 on which to free himself, a time when most of the keepers were attending court at the Old Bailey. Some days before he had found a small nail and by bending it against the stone floor got it into such a shape that he was able to pick the padlock that secured his chains to the staples fixed in the floor. The nail also unlocked his handcuffs. By sheer strength he now separated the chain that linked his legs; but he could not rid his ankles of the fetters, these he drew up to his knees and secured them to his garters, so they would not drag and rattle.

He then endeavoured to climb up the chimney but six feet up he was stopped by some iron bars. He got down from the chimney, and with a piece of broken chain picked out the mortar and removed the stone flag at the spot where the iron bars were fixed. Having overcome that obstacle he continued his climb up the chimney, taking with him one of the bars, about three feet long and an inch square, which proved a useful tool. With it he worked out several stones which gave him access from the chimney into the Red Room, a chamber situated over the Castle, which had not been occupied for seven years.

Using the iron bar he broke off the door lock of the Red Room in less than ten minutes and found himself in a passage leading to the chapel; here he was confronted with another door, this one bolted on the opposite side. Again he employed the iron bar to good effect; he picked out a stone from the wall beside the door, thrust his arm through the hole and pulled back the door bolt. He was now in the chapel.

He knew that his way to the lower leads, or roof, was through a door on the other side of the chapel. He climbed over the spiked grille that separated the prisoners' section from the rest, taking time to break off a spike for use as an additional tool. The second chapel door was very strong and secured by a huge lock. Night was falling and he had to work in semi-darkness. With his nail, iron bar, and chapel spike he forced the lock and opened the door.

In the passage, his way was barred by two other solid, iron-locked doors. It was full dark now and his task seemed well-nigh hopeless. Desperation drove him on. Using the iron bar as a lever, he wrenched the lock, box and staples from the doorpost. The last door, to his immense relief, was bolted on his side and he opened it easily. He was now on the roof, breathing the cool night air. However, it was a long way down to the ground. He decided to descend by way of the roof of Newgate's turner, a workman whose house adjoined the prison.

But he needed blankets with which to lower himself. This required him going back to the Castle, retracing his way through the maze of wrecked doors and down the chimney, a nerve-racking ordeal! What if the turnkeys came to view him. But they did not, considering him secure enough. Standing on the roof once more he tied the blankets together, fixed one end to the roof with the chapel spike, and lowered himself lightly on to the roof of the turner's house, thence to the ground. It was midnight, and he was free again. In hiding the next day he managed to rid himself of the leg irons.

As the most wanted, and the most talked-about man in London, Jack acted with supreme foolhardiness. A few nights after his great escape he broke into a shop in Monmouth Street and stole some fine clothes; he then raided a pawnbroker's and took a short sword with a silver hilt, rings, watches, snuff-boxes and other goods. Thus equipped like a gentleman, Jack the lad strutted about town, drinking too much and boasting of his latest escapade.

His riotous behaviour brought him to the attention of the watch; he was arrested and taken to Newgate where he was locked in the Middle Stone Room, adjoining the Castle, and was loaded with 300 pounds of chains. From then until his execution he was watched day and night. During this time he was visited by the King's painter, Sir James Thorn-

Jack chained to the floor of the Stone Room at Newgate from which he could not escape.

[90]

Jack has his portrait painted by Sir James Thornhill, the king's painter.

hill, who did a portrait of Jack. Hogarth also came and made his portrait. His Majesty, George I, curious about his wayward subject, sent for two prints of Sheppard, 'shewing the manner of his being chained to the floor in the Castle of Newgate and describing the manner in which he made his escape from thence on the 15th of October'.

Jack was one of the sights of London. 'Nothing contributes so much to the entertainment of the town at present,' commented a London journal, 'as the adventures of the housebreaker and gaolbreaker, John Sheppard. Tis thought the keepers of Newgate have got above £200 already by the crowds who daily flock to see him.' This time

[92]

there was no escape and on 16 November 1724 a mob of 200,000 turned out for his execution at Tyburn. He died in his twenty-third year and was buried in the churchyard of St Martin-in-the-Fields.

Two weeks after his hanging his dramatized story, *Harlequin Jack Sheppard* (the first of numerous plays and comedies based on his life) was performed at Drury Lane. Broadsheets and chapbooks telling his adventures sold like hotcakes, and an enterprising preacher in the city made good use of Jack's great escape, delivering a sermon to his respectable congregation that ended thus;

'Oh that ye were all like Jack Sheppard! Mistake me not, my brethren, I don't mean in a carnal, but a spiritual sense, for I purpose to spiritualise these things. What a shame it would be if we did not think it worth while to take as much pains, and employ as many deep thoughts, to save our souls, as he has done to preserve his body. Let me exhort you then to open the locks of your hearts with the *nail* of repentance; burst asunder the *fetters* of your beloved lusts; mount the *chimney* of hope; take from thence the *iron bar* of good resolution; break through the *stone wall* of despair, and all the strongholds in the *dark passage* of the shadow of death; raise yourself to the *leads* [roof] of devine meditation; fix the *blanket* of faith with the *spike* of the Church; let yourselves down to the *turner's house* of resignation and descend the steps of humility. So shall ye come to the door of deliverance from the prison of iniquity and escape the clutches of that old executioner, the Devil.'

To which we can only say, Amen!

[93]

Dick Turpin on his legendary
mare, Black Bess, jumping the
toll gate at Hornsey. Illustration
from *Turpin's Ride to York* (1839),
a ride he never made in real life.

CHAPTER EIGHT

The Real Dick Turpin

NOW WE COME to the most celebrated of all highwaymen, the dashing Dick Turpin, the bold bandit hero of countless stories, ballads, and highly imaginative biographies. The legendary Turpin is a handsome highwayman of the gentlemanly kind who rode his noble-hearted mare Black Bess on a marathon gallop from London to York in twelve hours to escape the law.

The real Dick Turpin was neither handsome, nor a gentleman. He did not own a horse called Black Bess, and never made the famous ride to York. However, he was notorious in his own lifetime, being reported in newspapers of the day as 'Turpin, the renowned butcher-highwayman'; not because he was particularly murderous, but because he was by trade a butcher.

Turpin's face was never committed to canvas or paper from life by an artist. The only reliable descriptions we have are those published in contemporary proclamations offering rewards for his capture;

'Richard Turpin, a butcher by trade, is a tall fresh coloured man, very much marked with the small pox, about 26 years of age, about five feet nine inches high, lived some time ago in Whitechapel and did lately lodge somewhere about Millbank, Westminster, wears a blue grey coat and a light natural wig.'

Many of the enduring myths and fanciful anecdotes about Turpin (still perpetuated in a factual sense by writers today) were first related in the *Life of Richard Turpin* by Richard Bayes and Others in Essex, a mixture of fact and fiction published in 1739, shortly after the highwayman

Another scene from Turpin's mythical ride to York. The brave Black Bess dies from exhaustion caused by the non-stop gallop.

was hanged at York the same year. The Turpin of romantic legend was firmly established by William Harrison Ainsworth, who made 'Dauntless Dick' the hero of his novel *Rookwood*, published in 1834, and therein gave a vivid description of his ride to York. But Ainsworth made no

[96]

claims to truth, he simply penned a rattling good yarn to please the public.

Several modern biographers have endeavoured to penetrate the mists of legend to put the record straight, the most notable and scholarly being Derek Barlow's *Dick Turpin and the Gregory Gang*, published in 1973. If not the hat-doffing gallant of the Duval ilk, neither was Turpin the 'coarse, illiterate boor' and the 'cowardly ruffian' that some critics held him to be.

The real Dick Turpin was no gentleman. He was known to hold female victims over a fire in order to make them reveal the whereabouts of hidden wealth.

He was rough and often brutal to his victims, he was quick on the trigger, he was moody and given to sudden acts of rashness. He could read and write, and it was his ability to write that brought him to the gallows (sooner than he might otherwise have done). He died with cool courage in the required manner of a true highwayman. The story of Turpin, the pock-marked butcher, is as interesting as any fictionalized account.

He was born at Hempstead, Essex, in 1705. His father, John Turpin, being at times a butcher and an innkeeper. Dick was taught to read and write by the Hempstead schoolmaster James Smith, and became an apprentice butcher. At the age of twenty-one he married Rose Palmer (or Elizabeth Millington, opinion is divided on this point) and opened his own butcher shop at Buckhurst Hill. Rather than buy his meat on the open market, Turpin relied on a regular supply from a notorious gang of deer-stealers who operated in Waltham Forest. When his involvement with the gang was discovered, he gave up the trade and left the area to keep a public house.

An honest life, apparently, did not appeal to Turpin and he became a leading member of the Essex Gang, or Gregory Gang, a brutal band of deer-stealers and housebreakers. The gang specialized in invading lonely farmhouses and isolated residences and maltreating the occupants to make them reveal the whereabouts of hidden money and valuables. Two of many such reports which appeared in the journals of the time will suffice to acquaint you with the wicked activities of Turpin and the Gregory Gang. The following from *Read's Weekly Journal* of 8 February 1735;

'On Saturday night last, about seven o'clock, five rogues entered the house of the Widow Shelley at Loughton in Essex, having pistols etc., and threatened to murder the old lady if she would not tell them where her money lay, which she obstinately refusing for some time, they threatened to lay her across the fire if she did not instantly tell them, which she would not do [it has been written elsewhere, and not without the ring of truth that Turpin said, 'God damn your blood, you old bitch, if you won't tell us I'll sit your arse on the grate.'] But her son being in the room, and threatened to be murdered, cried out he would tell them . . . and did, whereupon they went upstairs and took near £100, a silver tankard, and other plate, and all manner of household goods. They afterwards went into the cellar and drank several bottles of ale and wine and broiled some meat . . . while they were doing this, two of the gang went into Mr Turkles, a farmer's, who rents one end of the widow's house, and robbed him of above £20 and then they all went off, taking two of the farmer's horses to carry off their luggage.'

In the same month the *London Evening Post* reported;

'On Tuesday night, about eight o'clock, five villains came to the house ot Mr Lawrence, a farmer at Edgeware-bury, near Edgeware, in Middlesex, but the door being bolted they could not get in, so they went to the boy who was in the sheep-house and compelled him to call the maid, who opened the door, upon which they rushed in, bound the master, maid, and one man-servant, and swore they would murder all the family if they did not discover their money, etc. They trod the bedding under foot in case there should be money hidden in it, and took £10 in money, linen, etc., all they could lay hands on, broke the old man's head [with their pistols], dragged him about the house, emptied a kettle of [boiling] water from the fire over him . . . and [Samuel Gregory] ravished the maid, Dorothy Street, using her in a most barbarous manner, [and] they went off, leaving the family bound.'

The outrages committed by the Gregory Gang in Essex, Middlesex, Surrey and Kent brought forth a Royal Proclamation offering a reward of £50 for information leading to the arrest of any member ot the gang, and a free pardon for any of the gang who turned King's evidence. Peace officers surprised Turpin and several others in a tavern in Westminster; Turpin escaped by jumping out of a window but three of the gang were caught. John Wheeler turned King's evidence and sent his comrades, including the rapist

[99]

Sam Gregory, to the gallows. It was the end of the Gregory Gang, but not of Dick Turpin, he took to highway robbery with Thomas Rowden, a pewterer by trade.

Turpin's name now appeared regularly in the newspapers and journals. The *London Evening Post* of 12 July 1735 reported that two gentlemen were held up between Wandsworth and Barnes Common 'by two highwaymen supposed to be Turpin the butcher and Rowden the pewterer, the two remaining of Gregory's gang, who robbed them of their money ... dismounted them, made them pull off their horse's bridles, then turning them adrift they rode off towards Roehampton.'

The *Grub Street Journal* of 24 July 1735 informed its readers that a Mr Omar of Southwark had an unfortunate meeting, between Barnes Common and Wandsworth, with 'Turpin the butcher and another person; [Mr Omar] clapt spurs to his horse, but they coming up with him, obliged him to dismount, and Turpin suspecting that he knew him, would have shot him, but was prevented by the other, who pulled the pistol out of his hand.'

Turpin and Rowden were busy bandits, and impudent with it. The *Grub Street Journal* of 16 October 1735 reported that, 'For about six weeks past, Blackheath has been so infested by two highwaymen (supposed to be Rowden and Turpin) that 'tis dangerous for travellers to pass. On Thursday Turpin and Rowden had the insolence to ride through the City at noonday, and in Watling Street they were known by two or three porters, who had the courage to attack them; they were indifferently mounted and went towards the bridge, so 'tis thought are gone the Tonbridge Road.'

About this time Rowden parted from Turpin and Dick's new companion in crime was, according to Turpin mythology, a noted highwayman called Tom King. Their alleged meeting happened like this. Dick came upon a solitary rider, 'well mounted and appearing like a gentleman'. Turpin demanded his money at gunpoint, whereupon the man laughed and said; 'What, dog eat dog? Come, come, brother

[100]

Turpin's alleged meeting with
Tom King. He did not know that
King was also a highwayman.
The two robbers joined forces.

Turpin, if you don't know me, I know you, and shall be glad of your company.' The two robbers immediately formed an alliance. True or not, all we know for certain is that Turpin did associate with a highwayman named King.

The story goes that in March 1737 they established a hideout in a cave in Epping Forest, from which they sallied forth to rob travellers in the area. The *Country Journal* for 23 April 1737 reported that, as a gentleman of West Ham and others were travelling to Epping, 'the famous Turpin and a new companion of his came up and attacked the coach in order to rob it. The gentleman had a carbine in the coach, loaded with slugs, and seeing them come up, got it ready and presented it at Turpin . . . but it flashed in the pan, upon which says Turpin, "God damn you, you have missed me, but I won't you", and shot into the coach at him, but the ball missed him, passing between him and a lady in the coach; and then they rode off towards Ongar.'

According to Richard Bayes' *Life of Richard Turpin*, Dick and Tom King parted company in dramatic fashion. During a shoot-out with Bayes over a stolen horse, Turpin fired at Bayes, who was struggling with King, missed his man and

Dick shoots Tom King by mistake during a struggle with an inn-keeper over a stolen horse.

[102]

Dick in his hideaway cave in
Epping Forest.

[103]

killed his colleague instead. There are several versions of the incident, all of them confusing.

In early May 1737 Turpin's notoriety increased when he murdered a keeper of Epping Forest who tried to take him. As the armed keeper approached him, Turpin 'immediately discharged a carbine at him loaded with slugs, and shot him into the belly dead on the spot'. A Royal Proclamation was issued offering a reward of £200 (a very large sum in those days) for Turpin's arrest and described him thus; 'About

Turpin kills a keeper of Epping Forest outside his cave. For this murder a reward of £200 was placed on his head.

[104]

'Stand and deliver!' eighteenth century highwayman holds up a stage-coach.

The Hold Up, painting by
Charles M. Russell.

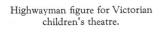

Highwayman figure for Victorian
children's theatre.

Your Obedient Servant by J. C.
Dollman, 1888. A highwayman
mockingly bows to his own
portrait on a reward poster.

thirty years of age, by trade a butcher, about five feet nine inches high, of a brown complexion, very much marked with the small pox, his cheek bones broad, his face thinner towards the bottom, his visage short, pretty upright, and broad about the shoulders.'

Despite the heavy price on his head, Turpin continued his depredations. One evening, at Holloway and in the back lanes of Islington, he held up several gentlemen in their coaches and carriages. When one of the victims made bold to mention to Turpin that he had reigned a long time, the *London Magazine* reported that Dick replied, 'Tis no matter for that. I'm not afraid of being taken by you, therefore don't stand hesitating, but give me the cole [money].'

In the mid-summer of 1737 Turpin departed his old haunts of London and Essex and established himself in

Dick holds up the York to London stage-coach, as imagined by a nineteenth century illustrator.

Yorkshire as a horse dealer (or, more accurately, a horse stealer) under the assumed name of John Palmer. Here he lived undetected until his rashness brought about his undoing. On returning to the town of Welton from an unsuccessful hunting expedition, he took the fancy to shoot his landlord's gamecock in the street. On being reproved by a Mr Hall, Turpin scowled at him and said, 'If you'll stay while I charge my piece, I'll shoot you, too.' Killing the cock was a foolish act but it could have been settled without further complications; the threat against Mr Hall was folly indeed.

Hall reported the incident to the landlord in question, who got out a warrant for apprehending the 'said Palmer'. Turpin was taken before the magistrates, who demanded sureties for his good behaviour, and as he could not produce them he was committed to the House of Correction. Suspicions deepened about Palmer and further investigations into his activities brought accusations of horse stealing, which led to his incarceration in York Castle in October 1738. But still the authorities did not know that he was the infamous Dick Turpin.

An act of folly that sent Turpin to the gallows. He shoots his landlord's gamecock and threatens to do the same to an onlooker. He lands in jail and his real identity is discovered.

[106]

From his cell he wrote to his brother-in-law at Hempstead. It is claimed that several letters were involved but as this is a matter of controversy, I shall cite only the one that is generally accepted, dated 6 February 1739:

> *Dear Brother,*
>
> *I am sorry to acquaint you that I am now under confinement in York Castle for horse stealing. If I could procure any evidence from London to give me a character, that would go a great way towards my being acquitted. I had not been long in this country before my being apprehended, so that it would pass off the readier. For heaven's sake, dear brother, do not neglect me; you will know what I mean when I say,*
>
> *I am, your's, John Palmer.*

The letter was not prepaid and Turpin's brother-in-law, for reasons not clear, refused to accept the letter and pay the sixpence postage demanded. The sealed letter was returned to the Hempstead post office, where it was seen by James Smith, the schoolmaster who had taught Turpin to read and write. Smith recognized the handwriting on the envelope and took it to a magsitrate, who opened it. Turpin's fate was sealed.

Smith went to York to identify Turpin and lay claim to the reward. At Dick's subsequent trial for horse stealing (a capital offence) he was also identified by another witness from Hempstead, Edward Saward, who had known him for many years. He was found guilty and sentenced to death. Had he not been identified as Turpin, it is likely that John Palmer would still have been found guilty of horse stealing; but the fact that he was the most wanted highwayman in England removed any doubt whatsoever from the minds of the jury that the pocked-marked accused was fit for the gallows.

In the tense period between sentence and execution, the undaunted Turpin enjoyed eating, drinking, and joking with the many visitors who came to see the celebrated highwayman, regaling them with stories of his adventures. Determined to go out in style, he bought new clothes and shoes in which to die, and paid five mourners, wearing black hat-bands and mourning gloves, to follow him to the gallows. He was executed on 7 April 1739, aged thirty-three. He died bravely, as the *York Courant* witnessed;

'Last Saturday, Richard Turpin and John Stead were executed at Tyburn for horse stealing. The latter died very penitent, but the former behaved with the greatest assurance to the very last: it was very remarkable, that as he mounted the ladder his right leg trembled, on which he stamped it down with an air, and with undaunted courage looked round about him, and after speaking a few words to the topsman [executioner], he threw himself off the ladder and expired in about five minutes.'

That was the end of Turpin the mortal man, and the beginning of Turpin the legend, handsome knight of the road, the immortal hero of countless ballads, books, plays and films.

CHAPTER NINE

Sixteen-string Jack

JOHN 'JACK' RANN, according to a contemporary description, was about 'five feet five inches high, wore his own hair, of a light brown colour, which he combed over his forehead, was remarkably clean and particularly neat in his dress, which in two instances was very singular, that of always having sixteen strings to his breeches knee, always of silk (by which means he acquired his fictitious name) and a remarkable hat with strings, and a button on the crown. He was straight, of a genteel carriage, and makes a very handsome appearance.'

Indeed, 'Sixteen-string Jack' was a dandy, a beau-bandit 'to be classed among the most impudent and arrogant self-created gentlemen who levied arbitrary contributions on the highway'. Fancy clothes and the desire to be regarded as a gentleman were the ruling passions of his short life.

Born near Bath around the middle of the eighteenth century, he first earned a living as a pedlar. On coming to London he obtained employment as a stable boy, progressed to the position of postchaise driver, and then an officer's batman. But the honest, humble life did not appeal to him. He developed a taste for fashionable clothes, fast women, and high living and required considerable money to indulge these fancies. So he turned to highway robbery.

His first reported brush with the law came in 1772 when he was charged with robbing a coach on Hounslow Heath. But Jack, who wore sober clothes and a mask on the job, was acquitted because the victims could not swear to his identity. He continued his career on the road and was careful not to deal direct when disposing of his plunder; this being done through an intermediary.

[109]

John Rann, alias Sixteen String Jack.

Jack took up with a young prostitute named Eleanor Roche. In May 1774 he held up John Devall near the nine-mile stone on the Hounslow road and took from him seven guineas and a watch. Eleanor Roche sent a girl called Catherine Smith with the watch to a pawnbroker, who became suspicious and informed the Bow Street Runners. Catherine led the law to Jack and Eleanor.

Jack was brought before Sir John Fielding, the blind Bow Street magistrate. The little highwayman was defiant in both dress and demeanour. 'His irons [shackles] were tied up and decorated with blue ribands, and he had a bundle of flowers affixed to the breast of his coat as large as a common birch-broom.' Jack denied everything. 'I know no more of the matter than you do', he told the magistrate.

Committed for trial, Jack and Eleanor answered the charge at the Old Bailey in July 1774. Again he generated an air of cocky self-confidence; his irons were decorated as before and he sported a flamboyant bouquet. He based his

[110]

defence on the premise that Catherine Smith was an unreliable witness, a spurned lover of his who was trying to do
him down; in other words she was trying to frame poor
Jack. The jury gave him the benefit of the doubt and Jack
and Eleanor were acquitted. Catherine Smith was also
discharged.

Four months later Jack again stood before Sir John
Fielding, on a charge of burglary. But this time he was
patently innocent. An old watchman had caught Jack
climbing through a window of a house at midnight. The
watchman had dragged him out by the silk-stockinged legs
and, refusing to listen to Jack's explanation, had detained
him until the following morning to appear at Bow Street.

[111]

Jack told Sir John that he had been late to keep an appointment with a girl named Doll Frampton; when he arrived at the house the girl had gone to bed, so he had decided to climb through the window and surprise her. Doll Frampton was called to give evidence and she corroborated Jack's story. Sir John Fielding had no option but to discharge the romantic robber.

Jack was now something of a celebrity and he revelled in the role. He appeared at a fashionable party, 'elegantly dressed in a scarlet coat, tambour [embroidered] waistcoat, white silk stockings, laced hat, etc.', and openly declared himself a highwayman. He drank a lot, became aggressive and a scuffle broke out, during which he lost a ring worth 100 guineas from his finger; however, he shrugged off the loss by boasting that he could easily replace its value with a single night's work on the road.

Jack was more upset by an affront to his dignity as a gentleman. When roughly arrested for debt by the sheriff's men, and released shortly afterwards when his friends paid the money, he complained to the sheriff; 'You have not treated me like a gentleman. When Sir John Fielding's people come after me they only hold up a finger, beckon, and I follow like a lamb. There's your proper civility!'

He was soon on the road again, but now he did not bother with discretion or disguise. The Bow Street Runners were always in pursuit. One evening he pulled up his horse at the turnpike at Tottenham Court Road and asked the tollman if anybody had been inquiring after him.

'No, why should they?' replied the tollman. 'Who are you, anyway?' Surprised by such ignorance, Jack exclaimed; 'What, you do not know me? I am Sixteen-string Jack, the famous highwayman. Have any of Sir John Fielding's people been this way?' By now the tollman had glimpsed Jack's pistols and he changed his tune. 'Yes', he said, 'some of them have just gone through.' To which Jack replied, 'Good, when you see them again tell them I am gone towards London.' And he galloped off in the opposite direction.

Jack at leisure strutted about like a peacock. At Barnet

races he appeared dressed 'like a sporting peer of the first rank' in a waistcoat of blue satin laced with silver and was followed 'by hundreds from one side of the course to the other, whose looks expressed their pleasure and satisfaction to behold a genius of whose exploits the world had talked so freely'.

But time was running out for our popinjay hero. He formed a partnership with a highwayman named William Collier, and in September 1774 they held up Dr William Bell on the Uxbridge Road and took from him a small amount of money and a watch. Eleanor Roche entrusted her servant to pawn the watch. The suspicious pawnbroker made enquiries that led to the final arrest of Jack Rann.

He stood trial at the Old Bailey, elegant as ever, 'dressed in a new suit of pea-green, his hat bound with silver strings; he wore a ruffled shirt, and his behaviour evidenced the utmost unconcern'. But this time the evidence against him was damning; both he and Collier were found guilty and sentenced to death. Eleanor Roche got fourteen years transportation for receiving stolen property. Collier was later reprieved and Jack alone paid the ultimate penalty.

He went out like a true-blue highwayman. His sang-froid never deserted him. On the eve of his execution he gave a lively dinner party in his Newgate cell, at which seven girls attended. On 30 November 1774 he faced the gallows at Tyburn with a flashy fortitude, wearing his pea-green suit and sixteen strings.

William Page, who flourished some twenty years before Jack Rann, was another stylish highwayman with a passion for extravagant clothes. Page was a farmer's son of Hampton, Middlesex, who came to London to learn the haberdashery business. Page quickly developed an inordinate fondness for fashionable attire. 'He was such a consummate coxcomb, that he was perpetually employing tailors to alter his clothes to any new fashion.' To pay the tailors he stole from the till and consequently lost his job.

He next took service with a wealthy gentleman as a livery-servant, and it was during a journey with his master that he

WILLIAM PAGE.

gained his first experience of highway robbery. A well-dressed, mounted highwayman held them up and Page's employer immediately shelled out a large amount of money. Thoroughly impressed by the robber's cool and profitable performance, Page decided to become a highwayman. He managed to procure a brace of pistols and a horse and set out on the plunderer's road.

His first foray brought him £4 from a lone traveller; it was enough to whet his appetite for bigger fish. His next expedition took him to Shooter's Hill, where he stopped the Canterbury coach, easing the passengers of their money and valuables to the value of £30. After that he rode through Kent reconnoitring the roads and approaches to London, gaining an intimate knowledge of the land that served him well, and he made himself an excellent map of the roads twenty miles around London. His operations were extensive and he soon acquired a considerable sum of money.

Page set himself up in fine rooms near Grosvenor Square, purchased a grand wardrobe of high fashion and got himself an elegant mistress. Although a bold and canny highwayman he was a sucker for the gaming tables and constantly had to replenish his coffers with raids on the

[114]

roads. Page was an innovator in the crime of highway robbery. Besides being a competent amateur cartographer, he travelled to 'work' in a handsome phaeton (light, open carriage) and pair, ostensibly a respectable gentleman out for a ride.

He would drive out of London, park the phaeton in a secluded place, change from his gentleman's attire into the dark clothes and mask of a highwayman, saddle one of the horses and ride off with his pistols primed to commit a robbery on the main road. This done, he hastened back to the phaeton, resumed his normal dress and drove back to

William Page holds up a traveller. The highwayman's carriage is parked in the background.

London. He was frequently cautioned by well-wishers on the road to be on his guard against one particularly daring highwayman – *himself*!

His boldness and quick-thinking are best illustrated by the following story. Having robbed some travellers near Putney, he returned to where he had concealed the phaeton and the remaining horse, and found they had gone. He followed the carriage tracks and discovered the vehicle had been taken by some haymakers, who were now apprehended as highwaymen by the irate travellers that Page had just robbed. On sizing up the situation, Page divested himself of his dark clothes and appeared on the scene in his underwear, claiming ownership of the phaeton and accusing the unfortunate haymakers of robbing and stripping him.

His recent victims readily sympathized with him and all parties went before the local justice of the peace. Page proved his ownership of the phaeton (having purchased it quite properly) and the haymakers were committed for trial. However, having got his carriage back and still unsuspected as a highwayman, Page did not appear to prosecute at the next assizes and the haymakers were acquitted for lack of evidence.

Page gave up using the phaeton and joined forces with a highwayman named Darwell. It was a successful partnership; in three years they committed some 300 robberies. But all the funds that Page gained by pillage he dissipated on high living and gambling. The end came when Darwell was caught and induced to turn King's evidence against his colleague. William Page was arrested, convicted, and hanged on 6 April 1758.

CHAPTER TEN

The Bushrangers of Australia

THE BUSHRANGING BANDITS of nineteenth-century Australia were very similar to the English breed of highwaymen of the eighteenth century. They rode fine horses, robbed stage-coaches with the demand 'Bail up!' and ambushed the gold escorts that transported the precious metal from the goldfields to the banks. And when they stood on the gallows, bushrangers mostly faced their end with bravado in the tradition set by the best English highwaymen.

However, the bushrangers were more violent, more ruthless than their British counterparts. Spawned in desperate circumstances they readily used their firearms to gain their loot or to escape capture. The first bushrangers were direct products of the harsh system of the prison colony. In 1788, Britain began transporting many of her convicted criminals to the newly discovered land. The idea was to give the felons a fresh start in helping to develop the colony. But they were ill-used from the beginning.

Their employers or masters believed in maintaining good order by free application of the lash. Floggings were administered for even trifling offences – drunkenness, disobedience, idleness and neglect of work. Cases were known of men who received, in aggregate, two or three thousand lashes. There was little or no alleviation of the convicts' hard lot, their only relaxation being to drink, gamble, quarrel and fight.

As the years passed and the convict population increased, other methods of containing them were introduced; the road working parties, the chain gangs, and the penal settlements. The chain gangs were kept mostly in the

[117]

interior, lodged in stockades, under a military commandant with soldier guards. The really hard cases were confined in penal settlements, such as the notorious Norfolk Island where, in the words of an eminent colonial judge, 'the heart of a man was taken from him, and he was given the heart of a beast'.

The more daring spirits among the convicts contrived to escape and took to the 'bush', or wild country where they robbed and killed travellers and preyed on lonely home-steads. When pursued by officers of the law, they preferred to shoot it out rather than be returned to captivity or face the gallows. Mostly they worked in small gangs under the command of various leaders they respected. They generally began their bushranging career by stealing good horses – racers by preference – on which they could make swift escapes from their pursuers.

'Summary Justice-Flogging a Bush Thief', illustration from *The Graphic* of 1883. It was this kind of inhuman treatment that caused many transported convicts to escape from the penal settlements and take up bushranging.

[118]

By the early 1820s bushrangers had become so numerous and bold that they robbed along the Parramatta Road to the very gates of Sydney, the chief town of Australia. Indeed, at that time the number of convictions for highway robbery in New South Wales alone was equal to the whole of the convictions for all crimes in the United Kingdom. To combat the growing menace Sir Thomas Brisbane, Governor of New South Wales, formed the mounted police and in 1822 hanged thirty-four of the pestilent highwaymen.

Paradoxically, the exploits of the bushrangers aroused as much admiration as fear among the settlers and public sentiment was often on their side, Australia being a young country where courage, audacity and self-reliance were considered among the highest virtues. This gave rise to the 'bush telegraph' or word-of-mouth communication in which the movements of the police, and the traps laid for the capture of the outlaws, were constantly frustrated by the rapidity of information conveyed to the bushrangers by their sympathizers.

One of the first of the legendary highwaymen was 'Bold' Jack Donahoe, the original 'Wild Colonial Boy' of the popular ballad. An Irishman, he was transported for life in 1824 at the age of eighteen. Three years later he took to the bush with two others. They were soon caught after 'bailing up' several bullock carts on the road to Richmond, a settlement near Sydney. All three were sentenced to hang, but Donahoe, albeit in chains, managed to escape. His two mates went to the gallows.

Jack returned to the bush, with a reward of £20 posted for him. He teamed up with a gang of eight and they raided widely, robbing travellers of money and valuables, stealing horses and cattle, and plundering homesteads for supplies. So notorious did the Donahoe gang become that a special police patrol was ordered to hunt them down. When the police did catch up with them, a gunfight ensued in which two of the outlaws were killed and three captured. But the daring Donahoe was not one of them, he managed to escape again.

Bushrangers attack the gold escort that transported the precious metal from the gold fields to Sydney.

He next ranged with several fugitives from the chain gang and they took to exchanging clothes with well-heeled coach travellers they held up; Donahoe and his mates became the best-dressed bushrangers around. Finally, in September 1830, Jack was surrounded by mounted police in a wooded spot some twenty-seven miles from Sydney.

[120]

Defiant to the end, two bullets ended the life of the wild colonial boy. Ballad makers soon turned him into a folk hero and the song *Bold Jack Donahoe* so offended the authorities that its singing was prohibited in the colony's beer shops and taverns.

William Westwood, known as 'Jackey Jackey' for some obscure reason, was another transported convict worker driven to the bush by his overseer's stockwhip. Transported at the age of sixteen for forgery, he was assigned to the Philip King estate where he later suffered a severe flogging. He ran off, joined with a fellow fugitive and raided first the estate whence he had escaped. Here he bound the brutal overseer to a tree and repaid him with a whipping.

Jackey Jackey earned a reputation as a gentleman highwayman; he robbed with courtesy, was particularly considerate to women, and never killed. He ranged in the Goulburn district, south-west of Sydney, and on the Bungendore Road, holding up travellers and raiding homesteads. He seems to have been influenced by the legendary Claude Duval for on one occasion he danced with a lady victim by the roadside. There are many stories, mostly apocryphal, of his reckless daring.

One tells of him, fashionably dressed, attending a ball given by the Governor of New South Wales, where he had the cheek to chat to the governor himself; having made a great impression on the ladies he departed the scene undetected. Jackey Jackey was eventually caught and sent to the hellish penal camp of Norfolk Island, where he led a revolt that was quickly crushed by troops. He was hanged in 1846.

Van Dieman's Land (Tasmania) was notorious for its harsh penal settlements, and many escapers bushranged across the island. A notable example was 'Gentleman Matt' Brady, a former valet from Manchester, transported for forgery. He ran away from the lash and the leg-irons in 1824 and formed a gang. They stole horses, robbed stagecoaches and farms and became such a thorough nuisance that a civil defence force was raised to help the soldiers and police combat the Brady boys.

When Lieutenant-Governor George Arthur offered a reward of £25 for each member of the gang, dead or alive, Brady retaliated by posting reward notices offering twenty-five gallons of rum for the capture of 'a person known as George Arthur'. Black trackers, always greatly feared by bushrangers, were brought over from the mainland to hunt down Brady, and they succeeded. His trial and subsequent hanging in Hobart in 1826 was well-attended by the gentry, who manifested much sympathy for the condemned man.

The second generation of bushrangers were for the most part free-born native Australians, some of them sons of former convicts. They took to the bush for excitement, sheer devilry, and the easy money to be had from 'bailing up' travellers and gold shipments. The discovery of gold in Australia in 1851 and the rush it generated brought a great increase in lawlessness. Bushrangers were everywhere. 'Robberies have now become so frequent that it is dangerous to travel or move about', announced a Sydney newspaper, 'A representation should be made to Government showing the unprotected state of life and property.'

But the authorities seemed powerless to check the bush-rangers. The police were spread thin over a wide area, the constables not always of a high calibre, and they often displayed a timidity in pursuing the armed and desperate bandits who knew the country like the back of their hands. *Bell's Life*, the popular sporting paper, poked fun at the feeble police with the following item, a common though wickedly reversed situation;

'Last evening three bushrangers espied a large body of troopers and immediately gave chase. The darkness of the evening favoured the escape of the troopers and baffled the bushrangers.'

However, the police had a considerable reason for their lack of success. The bushrangers were hard riders, well organized and led by enterprising young men; they enjoyed a great measure of support among the settlers, many of whom were kin of the outlaws, and the bush telegraph

alerted the bandits of approaching danger. In this sympathetic climate it is not surprising that the free-ranging highwaymen became bolder in their 'robberies under arms'.

Outstanding among the new generation of gold rush bushrangers was Frank Gardiner, who throughout the western and southern districts of New South Wales was hailed as the 'King of the Road'. Born in 1830 at Boro Creek, near Goulburn, son of a free settler, he started his criminal life at the age of nineteen by stealing horses. As a highwayman he led a gang that included Ben Hall, who later became a legend himself, and Johnny Gilbert, the 'Boy Bushranger'. It was Gardiner and his mates who 'bailed up' the gold escort at Eugowra Rocks, one of the great exploits of bushranger history.

Once a week a mail coach, guarded by troopers, and loaded with gold and paper money left Forbes, the chief centre of the Lachlan goldfields, for Sydney. On 15 June 1862 Frank Gardiner and his gang waylaid the gold escort

[123]

at Eugowra Rocks. As the coach rattled into the ambush, the robbers ruthlessly opened fire without warning, wounding two of the policemen; the coach horses bolted and the vehicle, hitting a boulder, overturned. The troopers departed hastily, leaving the bushrangers to plunder the coach of £12,000 in gold and banknotes.

A police patrol was soon on the trail of the bandits and Sergeant Sanderson (a fine man) and five troopers ran down Gardiner and four of the gang with part of the loot on a pack-horse. The outlaws galloped off, leaving the pack-horse behind. Sanderson did not pursue them further but returned to Forbes with half the stolen treasure.

Gardiner and his mistress went into hiding at Apis Creek, Queensland, running a tavern under assumed names, but the police eventually found them and they were taken to Sydney. Gardiner was sentenced to thirty-two years imprisonment and was released after serving ten, on condition that he left Australia. He went to San Francisco and never returned to his homeland.

Ben Hall was arrested for the gold escort job but released because of insufficient evidence. An incorrigible bushranger, he continued his raiding in company with Johnny Gilbert and Johnny Dunn. They plagued the Sydney–Melbourne Road. Between February 1863 and April 1865 Ben Hall and his mates robbed ten mail coaches, stole some twenty horses for their own use, and plundered numerous homesteads and stores.

In May 1865 Hall was betrayed to the police by an old comrade and troopers surrounded his camp at Billabong Creek, near Forbes.

> When the shadows broke and the dawn's white sword
> Swung over the mountain wall
> And a little wind blew over the ford
> A sergeant sprang to his feet and roared
> 'In the name of the Queen, Ben Hall.'
> (from the ballad, *The Death of Ben Hall*)

Hall refused to surrender and was shot dead, his body

Ben Hall, shown here in a contemporary illustration, was one of many bushrangers who have become Australian folk heroes. He died in a hail of police bullets in 1865.

riddled with fifteen bullets. Later, the police tracked down Johnny Gilbert and he too was killed in a gunfight. Johnny Dunn was wounded, captured, and hanged.

'Captain Thunderbolt' was the sobriquet of a famous bushranger named Frederick Ward. He was born at Windsor (New South Wales) in 1836 to respectable parents. Like most Australian lads of his time he grew up in the saddle. He first fell foul of the law for stealing a horse and was sentenced to a spell in Sydney's penal camp on Cockatoo Island. After suffering a number of floggings he escaped into the bush.

He soon became celebrated as a highwayman of the gallant type, treating his lady victims with courtesy, and always endeavouring to avoid personal injury to those he robbed. Full of derring-do he once, when pursued by the police, jumped his blood horse over a wide chasm and the gap is still known as Thunderbolt's Leap.

Ward's love of fine horses (he stole only the best) led to his eventual downfall. Having taken a thoroughbred in May 1870 he was reckless enough to ride it boldly and proudly through the town of Uralla, where he was spotted by two policemen, who gave chase. One of the officers was ridden into the ground but his comrade, Constable Walker pressed after the speeding bushranger.

[125]

Bold are the mounted robbers who on stolen horses ride
And hold the mounted troopers who patrol the Sydney
side
But few of them, though flash they be, can ride and
few can fight
As Walker did for life and death with Ward the other
night.
    (from the ballad, *A Day's Ride*)

Bushrangers were expert horsemen and rode only the best horses they could buy or steal.

At last Walker caught up with his man on the banks of a small lagoon. The outlaw plunged his horse into the water. Walker followed him and demanded his surrender. Ward refused, but did not shoot at the constable, instead he hurled himself upon the officer in order to drag him from the saddle. Walker shot him dead.

Francis McCallum, alias 'Captain Melville' was another gentleman bushranger, well-spoken and polite in 'bailing up' his victims. Born at Perth, Scotland, he was transported in 1838 for seven years for housebreaking while still a youth. A brave spirit, he was whipped and whacked but they could not break him. He escaped, was captured, received a further sentence and was finally released in 1849.

[126]

The thoroughbred stolen by
Captain Thunderbolt. His reckless
pride in riding the horse through
the town of Uralla led to his
downfall.

Sydney, capital of New South
Wales, as it looked in 1863.

He intended to dig for gold, instead he turned to robbing
the diggers and plagued the roads between Melbourne and
the goldfields. He ended his own life by committing suicide
in jail after his capture.

Head and shoulders above all bushrangers stands Ned Kelly, Australia's major folk hero. Part Robin Hood, part ruffian, he was a controversial figure in his own time and remains so today. The view of many was and is that he was a high-spirited lad, wild but not wicked, persecuted by the police over petty matters until he became a 'forced outlaw', as he described himself in a letter to a leading politician; Ned was as competent with a pen as he was with a gun.

In another environment, with a better start in life, Ned Kelly might have become a leading citizen, or a prosperous farmer, for he certainly had the intelligence and determination to succeed. Perhaps so, what he did become was a killer and a robber. His fame rests largely on his remarkable 'Last Stand', a dramatic gunfight with the police in which he wore home-made armour and a helmet similar to that worn by a medieval knight. This aspect alone marks the 'Iron Bushranger' as notable among his fellow brothers-in-arms.

Edward 'Ned' Kelly was born in June 1855 in a primitive cabin at Beveridge, some twenty-five miles from Melbourne, in the colony of Victoria. His father, John 'Red' Kelly was a former convict, born in Ireland and transported in 1841 for seven years for stealing two pigs. After serving his time, John Kelly settled in the new land, renting a small farm. He married the daughter of James Quinn, a free settler from Ireland.

The Kellys and the Quinns were many, they and their friends and sympathizers inhabited what the police came to call 'Kelly Country', a close-knit community in which the police were unwelcome and the bush telegraph was swift and efficient. Ned grew up among rough men who saw little wrong in stealing horses and cattle when they needed them. Several of his uncles, and his father, were jailed for this kind of activity. Red Kelly died in 1866 shortly after his release. His father's death and his subsequent brushes with the law hardened young Ned's hostility towards the police.

At the age of fourteen Ned was a big fellow, tough as

V. R.

£1,000 REWARD!!!
FOR THE KELLY GANG.

GO AND SEE
THE GREAT PICTURE
OF THE
NOTORIOUS BUSHRANGERS,
Painted by Fry from a photograph taken on the ground where the Murder of Sergeant Kennedy was committed.
Every Visitor will be presented with a photograph of the Notorious Ned Kelly.
Now on View opposite Theatre Royal.

nails, a crackshot, and one of the best horsemen and bushmen in the district. In 1870, when he was fifteen, Ned was arrested on two counts of robbery under arms, being charged as the accomplice of the notorious bushranger Harry Power. It appears that the charges were justified but young Ned was acquitted on insufficient evidence. The local

[130]

police were now determined to knock the 'flashness' out of the embryo bushranger. In 1877, following further scrapes with the law, a drunken Ned got into a fight with four policemen; during this fracas Constable Lonigan earned Ned's undying enmity: 'I've never shot a man yet, Lonigan', he said, 'but if I ever do, you'll be the first.' Ned was a man of his word.

In April 1878 Constable Fitzpatrick (who, in an official report was described as 'not a fit person to be in the police force' and was later discharged) claimed that Ned Kelly had shot and wounded him, and for this alleged attack – which everyone knew to be untrue – Ned and his young brother Dan were outlawed, with a reward of £100 on their heads, dead or alive. The Kelly boys went on the run, joined by their friends Steve Hart and Joe Byrne. A four-man police party went after the gang and made camp at Stringybark Creek.

Ned and his mates approached the camp when two of the officers were away trailing. The two remaining constables were McIntyre and Lonigan. When Ned ordered them to raise their hands, Lonigan went for his gun. Ned shot him dead. The two other officers, Sergeant Kennedy and Constable Scanlon returned at dusk and on being told to surrender, they opened fire. Ned killed Scanlon with one shot and then Kennedy. Meanwhile, McIntyre had grabbed a horse and escaped.

The Stringybark killings branded Ned Kelly as a ruthless gunman. For his part, Ned wrote in a long letter to a member of Parliament, that killing the policemen 'cannot be called wilful murder for I was compelled to shoot them in my own defence or lie down like a cur and die'. The Victoria government proclaimed that any member of the gang could be shot by police and civilians. The reward for each gang member rose from £500 to £1,000 and then £2,000; in 1879 the sum was raised to £8,000.

In December 1878 the Kelly gang rode into Euroa, a small town in north-eastern Victoria, and robbed the National Bank of some £2,000 in cash and gold; Ned later

Ned kills Constable Lonigan and two other policemen at Stringybark Creek.

shared the plunder with his relatives and poor neighbours in the Kelly Country. In February 1879 the four bushrangers, each riding a stolen racehorse, crossed the border into New South Wales to raid the small town of Jerilderie.

First they surprised the town's police force of two constables and locked them up in their own jail. Dan Kelly and Joe Byrne put on the police uniforms and posed as members of a special patrol 'on their way to Victoria to help hunt for the Kellys'. Ned and 'Constable' Byrne entered the bank and held it up, taking £2,000 in cash. As they were leaving, the local schoolmaster walked in to withdraw some money. 'You're too late, mate', Ned said. 'Ned Kelly has just withdrawn the lot.'

With the town subdued, the bushrangers now proceeded to 'hurrah' the place in Wild West fashion. They treated everyone to drinks in the Royal Mail Hotel, and those that were reluctant were forced to drink to the Kelly gang at gunpoint. Ned delivered a speech on police persecution and the like. Finally, after an exhibition of horsemanship by Ned and Joe Byrne, the bushrangers rode out of the town, whooping and firing shots into the air. It was, say the citizens of Jerilderie, the most exciting thing that ever happened in the place.

As the hunt for the Kelly gang intensified, Ned knew that a final confrontation with the police was coming, and he prepared for it. Obtaining a quantity of cast iron plates, the gang fashioned them into crude body armour, covering the chest and back, but leaving the arms and legs unprotected. Only Ned had the addition of a helmet; his total armour weighed nearly 100 pounds.

On learning that a special train carrying a large force of police and the hated black trackers was on its way to scour the Kelly Country, Ned decided to capture the station of Glenrowan and rip up a section of the track to derail the

The police attack the Kelly Gang at Glenrowan following the gang's abortive attempt to derail a train.

train. Having established the ambush, the outlaws waited in the Glenrowan Hotel. But the police train failed to arrive at the expected time. 'Something's gone wrong', said Dan Kelly, and he suggested that they leave the place. 'I'm tired of running', Ned replied. 'We'll stand and fight.'

Ned Kelly, the 'Iron Bushranger', in his home-made armour.

In the meantime the train was alerted and stopped and the police approached the Glenrowan Hotel. Inside the timber building the four bushrangers buckled on their armour. It was three o'clock on the morning of 28 June 1880. In the gunfight that ensued, Joe Byrne was shot dead. Ned clanked out of the back of the hotel with the intention of attacking the police from the rear. When he appeared, a dozen officers concentrated their fire on the amazing iron-clad figure. 'Fire away', Ned cried defiantly. 'You can't hurt me.'

> The bullets bounced off him just like a stone wall
> His fiendish appearance soon did them appal
> His legs unprotected a trooper then found
> And a shot well directed brought him to the ground.
> (From the ballad, *The Kelly Gang*)

It was in fact a Sergeant Steele who finally felled Ned with a shotgun blast in his legs, and then disarmed him. Dan Kelly and Steve Hart still held out in the hotel. The police set fire to the flimsy building and the two young bush-rangers died in the flames.

[134]

Ned Kelly's last stand at Glenrowan. The police brought him down by shooting at his unprotected legs.

Ned Kelly as he looked a few days before his execution in 1880. His last words on the scaffold were 'Such is life'.

Ned Kelly recovered from his wounds and stood trial in Melbourne; he was found guilty of wilful murder and was hanged on 11 November 1880. 'Mind you die like a Kelly', his mother had told him on the eve of his execution, and he did, with fortitude. His last words, just before the trap fell beneath him, being, 'Such is life.'

[135]

CHAPTER ELEVEN

The Road Agents of America

DURING THE HEYDAY of highwaymen in England, highway robbery was scarcely known in the distant American colonies. In *Stagecoach and Tavern Days* Alice Morse Earle gives 'one very good reason why there was little highway robbery in America. Early in our history men began to use drafts and bills of exchange, where the old world clung to cash. English travellers persisted in carrying gold and banknotes, while we carried cheques and letters of credit.'

However, as the Americans moved West into the wide open spaces during the nineteenth century, and gold was discovered in California and elsewhere, stage-coach lines were plagued with highwaymen or 'road agents', as they were called. There were few lawmen out West and the wilderness proved ideal bandit country. Later, when the railroad introduced a new kind of highway through the wild regions, American outlaws such as Jesse James took to holding up and robbing trains.

One of the earliest examples of highway robbery in the English manner occurred in 1818 when the mail-coach which ran between Baltimore and Philadelphia was held up by Joseph T. Hare and his gang. One of the victims, Thomas Ludlow, wrote a report of the crime to the coach-owner in which he recorded that, 'About 2 miles from this place [Havre de Grace] the driver of your mail wagon and myself were attacked by three highwaymen, each armed with a double-barrelled pistol and a dirk. They had, previous to our arrival, built a rail fence across the road, and immediately on our driving up they leaped from behind the

[136]

same, where they lay concealed, and presented their pistols, threatening to blow out our brains if we made any resistance.'

The raiders got away with 15,000 dollars, but Joseph Hare was soon caught in Baltimore, while buying a fine plaid coat. He and another of his gang, John Alexander, were publicly hanged in September 1818. Just before he was 'turned off' Hare made the confessional boast that 'for the last fourteen years of my life I have been a robber on a large scale, and been more successful than any robber either in Europe or in this country that I ever heard of'. Just as in England, a chapbook was soon on the market entitled *The Life of the Celebrated Mail Robber and Daring Highwayman Joseph Thompson Hare*, and no doubt it sold well.

While Hare was standing trial for the mail-coach job, an Irishman named Michael Martin landed at Salem, Massachusetts. Possessing some capital, he set himself up in the business of brewer. But the enterprise failed and he returned to the trade in which he had been successful in the old country, that of highway robbery. For Michael Martin was none other than 'Captain Lightfoot', the former lieutenant of 'Captain Thunderbolt', Ireland's most notorious highwayman.

Born in 1775 near Kilkenny, Martin ran away from a cruel father and in Dublin met up with a powerfully built clergyman named John Doherty (a man of many parts), who revealed himself to young Michael as Captain Thunderbolt. Soon the two of them were robbing together, Doherty having dubbed his apprentice Captain Lightfoot. They preyed on travellers in Ireland and Scotland and when the highways became too hot for them they fled to America. In the new world they both decided to adopt an honest way of life. Doherty became a respectable doctor in Vermont (and remained so), but Martin reverted to his old profession.

He first robbed a Connecticut peddler of seventy dollars and with this bought himself a road agent's rig; a swift horse, a brace of pistols, and a dark Quaker suit. Over the next few years he became notorious throughout New

[137]

England. It is said that he robbed with good manners and was respectful to women. When a young female victim offered him her watch, he gallantly refused to take it, saying, 'Ma'am, I do not rob ladies.' Captain Lightfoot was captured, made a desperate jail break, was recaptured and hanged in Cambridge in December 1822.

The stage-coaches of the Old West were especially vulnerable to gangs of highwaymen who lay in wait on lonely trails. Robbery was most frequent in the Rocky Mountains, the Black Hills of Dakota, and the Pacific Coast regions where the gold and silver mines were located and where travellers usually carried large sums of money. On holding up a stage, the road agent's usual demand was 'Throw down the box!' – the steel strongbox in which precious metal and money were locked.

Ben Holladay, the tough, ruthless boss of the Holladay Overland Mail & Express Company was himself stopped and robbed by highwaymen. It was his favourite story, not least because he came out best in the encounter. Holladay's splendid Concord coach pulled by six handsome greys was

[138]

Chapbook relating the 'true' life and adventures of highwayman Joseph T. Hare, hanged in 1818.

held up near Denver, Colorado. The bandits relieved Ben of several hundred dollars pocket money and his large gold watch, which had a five-pound chain forged from gold nuggets. The road agents made off, well pleased with their plunder. But Holladay, although angry at the humiliation, had the last laugh. Dazzled by the watch, the robbers had missed the money belt, containing 40,000 dollars, which Ben wore next to his skin.

The Wild West in the latter half of the nineteenth century was infested with highwaymen. They sometimes pretended to be Indians in order to shift the blame for their depredations. Ralph Moody in *Stagecoach West* tells us that;

Typical stage-coach that travelled the dusty trails of the Wild West. This one is crossing the San Marcos Pass in California.

'It soon became evident that many crimes for which the Sioux had been blamed were actually committed by white men in disguise. Two [stage] men were killed and the mail sacks plundered in an attack north of Fort Laramie. Both men were scalped in Sioux fashion, but only the registered mail was plundered from the sacks.'

The Western Stage Company of Nebraska suffered so much from the road agents that it introduced a special security coach known as the 'Iron Clad' – a gold-carrying Concord armoured with bullet-proof steel plates, locked doors with narrow firearm ports, and a steel safe bolted to the floor inside the coach, guarded by a crackshot team of riflemen. The bandit-proof Iron Clad proved a great success.

The Wells Fargo company, in particular, was generous in its gratitude to the brave drivers and messengers who successfully fought off or captured highwaymen. When James W. Miller saved a 30,000-dollar payroll shipment from attempted hold-up in the 1860s, he was awarded a fine watch, encased in two pounds of Nevada silver. Stephen Venard, after killing three road agents who held up and robbed the North San Juan coach, was awarded 3,000 dollars and a handsome Henry (repeating) rifle engraved with a picture of the exploit and the inscription; 'Presented by Wells Fargo & Co. to Stephen Venard for his gallant conduct, May 16, 1866.'

In an article in *Harper's New Monthly Magazine* of July 1880, the writer describes a hold-up that happened on the trail between Las Vegas and Santa Fe, New Mexico;

'The first thing that I saw was four masked faces and eight revolvers belonging to men behind those rocks. Of course they "had the drop" on us, and we had to throw up our hands. And then they made us all get out, and they put the one lady passenger on one side, and then made the rest of us sit down on a log. One man kept the revolvers pointed at the party, and the others just "went through us" and took everything that we had in the world. The lady had some money but they left her alone.

'One fellow – a doctor – walked about, and the man with the revolver told him just to sit down on the log again. "Is it any of your business whether I sit or stand?" asked he. "Oh, no", said the highwayman pleasantly, "none at all, only I'll let daylight through ye if ye don't sit down – quick!" And he sat down. When they'd taken everything, even fifty-seven dollars of the driver's hard earnings – and they generally let them alone – they told us to keep still for twenty minutes, at peril of our lives, and took the horses and a buggy that they had up there among the trees, and went off.'

Of the numerous highwaymen that infested the Old West, 'Black Bart' was the most celebrated. Where others operated in pairs or in gangs, he always worked alone. Black Bart was unique in several ways. He robbed only Wells Fargo stage-coaches, a total of twenty-eight before his career was brought to an end in 1883. It appears that he never killed or injured anyone during his hold-ups. And he had a penchant for writing doggerel, leaving pieces of his verse in the looted strong boxes.

[142]

The road agent's view of his victims. A posed photograph of a hold-up.

Bart committed his first robbery in July 1875 when he stopped the regular stage from Sonora to Copperopolis in California. A tall figure in a linen duster coat with a flour sack mask over his head, aimed a double-barrelled shotgun at the driver and in a deep, well-modulated voice demanded, 'Throw down the box!' As the driver dropped the Wells Fargo strongbox, the robber called out to his hidden accomplices, 'Keep your eyes on the passengers, boys, if one of them dares to shoot, give them a solid volley.' Later, the driver reported that he had seen about a dozen shotguns poking through the bushes by the roadside.

During the hold-up a nervous woman passenger threw her purse out of the window in order to placate the robber. Black Bart picked it up and handed it back with studied courtesy, saying, 'Madam, I do not wish your money. In that respect, I honour only the good office of Wells Fargo.' Having also taken the mail sacks from the back boot of the

[143]

Rough highwaymen of California robbing their victims of money and personal jewellery, including earrings.

More road agents at work. Although they robbed passengers of everything of value, they seldom robbed the coach driver.

[144]

When a highwayman attempted to stop the coach *en route* from Denver City to Idaho Springs in 1878, he received a hot welcome from the three lady passengers, one of them a German baroness. The ladies put the robber to flight.

'Four road-agents overpower and plunder two officers and seven soldiers near Bismarck, Dakota Territory', from New York *Illustrated Times* of 1879.

[145]

coach, Bart ordered the driver to 'Hurry along now, my friend, and good luck to you.'

When James B. Hume, chief of Wells Fargo's detective force, was informed of the robbery he immediately offered a reward for any of the gang and hurried to the scene of the crime. Nearby he found the empty strongbox and mail sacks, the latter slit open in the form of a 'T'. In the bushes by the roadside he found a dozen sticks poking through the bushes, the supposed shotguns of the phantom gang that had backed up the bold bandit. Hume was now on the trail of a lone highwayman, six feet tall, who spoke excellent English in a deep, booming voice. But it would be a long time before he captured his man.

Five months later another stage was robbed. The *modus operandi* was the same. The road agent wore a linen duster and flour sack mask, sticks simulating shotguns poked through the bushes, and the mail bags were slashed open in the form of a 'T'. In June 1876 a similar robbery occurred. Then, in August 1877, Black Bart left the first of his mocking verses. A Wells Fargo circular offering 800 dollars reward for the arrest of the stage robber, stated;

'On the 3rd of August 1877, the stage from Fort Ross to Russian River was stopped by one man, who took the Express box [containing] about $300 in coin, and a check for $305.52 on Grangers' Bank of San Francisco, in favor of Fisk Bros. The Mail was also robbed. On one of the Way Bills left with the box the robber wrote as follows:

> I've labored long and hard for bread
> For Honor and for riches
> But on my corns too long you've tred
> You fine haired sons of bitches
>   BLACK BART, the P o 8 [the poet].

The hold-ups continued and James Hume was no nearer to catching Black Bart. In July 1878 the elusive highwayman robbed the stage from Quincy to Oroville of the Wells Fargo box, containing 379 dollars in coin, a diamond ring and silver watch. When the empty box was

$2500
REWARD

**On Sunday night, 27th inst., the
Stage from Colfax to Grass Valley
was stopped by four highwaymen and our
treasure box robbed of following amounts:**

$7.000 IN COIN.

**In a leather pouch, and three packages of
coin containing respectively $50, $18
and $10. We will pay the above**

REWARD OF $2500

**in Gold Coin for the capture of the robbers
and the recovery of the Coin; or**

$1250 FOR THE CAPTURE
of the Robbers, and

$1250 FOR THE RECOVERY
Of the Coin.

L. F. ROWELL,
Ass't. Supt. of Wells, Fargo & Co.

found next day, it held an extended version of the first
piece of doggerel;

> Here I lay me down to sleep
> To wait the coming morrow
> Perhaps success, perhaps defeat
> And everlasting sorrow . . .
> Let come what will, I'll try it on
> My condition can't be worse
> And if there's money in that box
> Tis munney in my purse
>   BLACK BART, the P o 8.

As the robberies continued in regular fashion the California newspapers demanded that the 'bloodthirsty criminal'
be caught and hanged. Criminal he certainly was, but

[147]

Charles E. Bolton, alias 'Black Bart', robbed a total of 28 Wells Fargo stage-coaches. He always worked alone and sometimes left a taunting verse in the plundered treasure box.

[148]

bloodthirsty never; Black Bart had never killed or injured
anyone. During 1881 and 1882 he held up ten stage-coaches
and during one robbery a brave driver caught a glimpse of
the mystery man beneath the flour sack. The driver
managed to bring his shotgun into action and, although he
just failed to hit Black Bart, the near-miss swept off his
sack mask and the bowler hat which made him appear six
feet tall. The driver reported that the highwayman was
about five feet eight, with grey hair and a large, white
moustache. James Hume was now looking for a smaller,
older man.

[149]

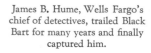

Black Bart's final hold-up ended with bloodshed, his own. On 3 November 1883 he stopped the stage out of Tuttletown. This time the Wells Fargo box, containing nearly 5,000 dollars in gold, was bolted to the floor of the coach, which was not carrying passengers. As Bart smashed open the strongbox inside the coach, the driver managed to get hold of a rifle; he fired at the robber but missed. Bart did not shoot back, he fled for cover in the bushes, carrying the loot. More shots were fired at him and he was wounded in the hand.

In his hasty escape, he dropped several personal items, among them a handkerchief with the laundry mark F.X.0.7 in indelible ink. This provided James Hume with the vital clue he needed. The detective had a notion that Black Bart lived in San Francisco and after some ninety laundries in the city had been checked it was discovered that the handkerchief belonged to Charles E. Bolton (or Boles, his real name is not certain), a well-spoken gentleman of some fifty years, five feet eight inches tall, with grey hair and a large white moustache.

When Black Bart was confronted, he made a deal with Hume and led the detective to where he had hidden the 4,815 dollars, the full amount he had stolen from the Wells

[150]

Fargo box. Charged with that crime only, Bart pleaded guilty before the California Superior Court and was sentenced to six years in San Quentin. He was released in 1888 and then vanished.

As the railroads reached out West, daring highwaymen turned to robbing trains. Holding up a stage-coach is one thing, but stopping a train in order to plunder it is quite another. The first train robbery in the United States is generally credited to the Reno gang of raiders. On 6 October 1866 the gang, led by the ruthless Reno brothers, flagged down a train on the Ohio & Mississippi Railroad as it slowed for a curve near Seymour, Indiana. They broke into the Adams Express car (a locked and guarded security wagon usually positioned immediately behind the locomotive and tender) and got away with some 10,000 dollars.

Two years later the gang struck again when they robbed the express car of a Jefferson, Madison & Indianapolis train at Northfield, a wood and water stop in Indiana. As the

[151]

THE ADAMS EXPRESS C.o

THIS COMPANY HAS FACILITIES UNSURPASSED BY THOSE OF ANY OTHER EXPRESS LINE IN THE WORLD, FOR THE SAFE & EXPEDITIOUS FORWARDING & PROMPT DELIVERY OF

BANK-NOTES, GOLD & SILVER COIN, PARCELS, PACKAGES, FREIGHT, &c.

.SO, FOR THE COLLECTION OF NOTES, DRAFTS & ACCOUNTS, IN ALL THE CITIES, TOWNS & VILLAGES IN THE EASTERN, WESTERN, SOUTHERN & SOUTH-WESTERN STATE

train pulled to a halt, the bandits overpowered the engineer (driver) and fireman; when the armed conductor came to investigate he was shot and severely wounded.

The outlaws uncoupled the engine, tender, and express car from the passenger coaches and steamed away into the night. Frank Reno and two others crawled along the roof of the speeding express car, reached the platform and broke open the door. The armed messenger inside was swiftly subdued and the merciless robbers threw him overboard as the train sped on. The three men smashed open the iron strongboxes and stole 97,000 dollars in gold and government bonds. The gang abandoned the hijacked train near Seymour, where they had horses waiting.

Like the Wells Fargo treasure box, the Adams Express Company's Car was a popular target for railroad robbers.

[152]

As protectors of the Adams Express Company (at that time the nation's major public carrier), the Pinkerton National Detective Agency went after the Reno gang. On learning that the outlaws planned to rob a train transporting 100,000 dollars in gold, Alan Pinkerton switched the shipment to another train. When the robbers broke into the original express car they were welcomed by a volley of gunfire from Pinkerton, his son William, and a posse. The Renos fled, several of the gang were wounded. Finally, Pinkerton agents rounded up the Reno brothers Frank, William and Simeon and handed them over to the law in New Albany, Indiana.

Robbing trains had brought the Renos fame, and a train brought them violent death. Just before midnight on 12 December 1868 a trainload of vigilantes left Seymour and pulled into New Albany early the following morning. The masked avengers stormed the jail, overpowered the sheriff and his staff and lynched the three Renos. With their grisly task completed, the vigilantes boarded the death train and returned to their homes.

Jesse James, America's so-called Robin Hood, secured his legendary fame by robbing banks and trains; he also held up stage-coaches in true highwayman fashion. In September 1880 he and a confederate, both mounted on fine horses, held up two stages in one day. The first netted them a reputed 700 dollars, the second nearly 2,000 dollars.

Jesse James, robber of banks, stage-coaches and trains.

[154]

Although there is no evidence that Jesse James distributed his plunder among the poor, it is not difficult to grasp why he was viewed by simple country folk as a kind of Robin Hood. For he robbed the banks and the railroads, large, heartless organizations for which the little farmer and poor folk had no love. In truth Jesse was a cold killer, more akin to the real Dick Turpin than the mythical Robin Hood. But a sympathetic Press, his treacherous assassination, and the dime novelists and ballad-makers transformed him into a folk hero, a good boy forced into outlawry.

Born in Missouri in 1847, Jesse and his elder brother Frank were farmboys who learned to kill and rob as members of the Confederate guerrilla band led by the infamous William Clarke Quantrill in the Civil War. When

The James Gang robbing an express car.

[155]

the war ended in 1865 Jesse rode in to surrender under a flag of truce and was shot and seriously wounded by a Union soldier. Perhaps it was this incident that hardened his soul and turned him into an outlaw.

The James Gang relieving passengers of their money and valuables.

He and Frank teamed up with Cole and Jim Younger and some others and they committed their first peacetime robbery in February 1866, when they raided a bank in Liberty, Missouri. The first railroad robbery carried out by the James-Younger gang took place in July 1873 when they derailed a train near Council Bluffs, Iowa, by removing part of the track. The locomotive overturned and the engineer died in the crash. The raiders charged the train, shooting and yelling as they did so. Having robbed the express safe of 2,000 dollars, they passed through the passenger cars and relieved the frightened travellers of their money and valuables.

In January 1874 the James-Younger gang held up another train, the Little Rock Express, at Gad's Hill, a tiny

[156]

Reward notice on the James Gang for railroad robbery and the murder of train conductor William Westfall. It is said that Jesse himself shot the man.

PROCLAMATION
$5,000⁰⁰
REWARD

FOR EACH of SEVEN ROBBERS of THE TRAIN at WINSTON, MO., JULY 15, 1881, and THE MURDER of CONDUCTER WESTFALL

$ 5,000,00
ADDITIONAL for ARREST or CAPTURE

DEAD OR ALIVE
OF JESSE OR FRANK JAMES

THIS NOTICE TAKES the PLACE of ALL PREVIOUS REWARD NOTICES.
CONTACT SHERIFF, DAVIESS COUNTY, MISSOURI
IMMEDIATELY
T. T. CRITTENDEN, GOVERNOR
STATE OF MISSOURI
JULY 26. 1881

[157]

hamlet in Wayne County, Missouri. This time the operation was notable for its imagination and lack of violence. Gad's Hill (named after Gad's Hill in England, on the Dover Road, a favoured hold-up spot for highwaymen) was a flag stop, that is to say the train stopped only if flagged down by a railroad agent or if a passenger wished to get off. The following account is based on *Missouri's First Train Robbery* by M. C. Eden, published in *The Brand Book* of January 1974 by The English Westerners' Society.

The robbers rode into Gad's Hill, captured the railroad agent, and as the train approached signalled it to stop with a red flag. They also threw the points switch that directed the slowing train off the main line on to a spur track; when the train ran on to the spur, the bandits moved the switch again so that the train could not reverse on to the main track. It was now safely isolated for plundering. As the conductor alighted to see what was happening, a masked gunman ordered him to 'Stand still, or I'll blow your head off.'

The road agents entered the express car, forced the messenger to give up his pistol, and proceeded to loot the safe of 1,000 dollars. On leaving the car, one of the masked raiders wrote in the messenger's receipt book; 'Robbed at Gad's Hill.' Jesse James was known to have a wry sense of humour. Then the gang passed through the rest of the train, robbing the passengers one by one. Having held the train for forty minutes, the outlaws galloped off and the plundered train continued to Piedmont, seven miles away, where a posse was raised and gave chase with no result.

In those days travelling by train through Jesse James country was fraught with danger. Robert J. Wybrow, a noted researcher and writer on the James gang, recently published the following letter, dated 1879, in which a mother warns her daughter of the hazards of railroad travel;

'Dear Daughter, the Chicago & Alton Railroad was robbed 3 miles south of Independence [Missouri] the other day. The robbers took all the money & valuables from all the passengers, took the rings off the ladies fingers &

[158]

earrings out of their ears. They took about 10,000 [dollars] in all. Three of the robbers called themselves Jesse James, [but] it is thought they were not the James. You had better be careful when you come home. Don't wear any jewellery, don't have only a little money in your jacket, put the rest in a pocket that they can't well reach, put it under all your

[159]

clothing all the jewellery you have. They said they intend robbing the road again. One man [a passenger] had a basket with a puppy in it, he stuffed his watch & pocket book [wallet] in the basket under the dog and they did not find it. Some hid their's under the carpet and one put [it] in his shoes. [signed] Mamma.'

Jesse James continued to rob banks, trains, and stage-coaches until he met his death in 1882 at the treacherous hands of one of his gang, Bob Ford, who shot Jesse in the back in his home at St Joseph, Missouri, for the reward money. Such is the occupational hazard of highwaymen and outlaws.

Butch Cassidy and the 'Wild Bunch' were another celebrated bunch of bandits who specialized in railroad robbery; their depredations spanned the nineteenth and twentieth centuries. The Wild Bunch, apparently, was so named from their boisterous antics in spending their loot.

Butch Cassidy and the 'Wild Bunch' specialized in robbing trains. Front row, left to right: Harry Longbaugh ('Sundance Kid'), Ben Kilpatrick, Robert Leroy Parker ('Butch Cassidy'). Back row: Bill Carver, Harvey Logan.

[160]

Butch Cassidy, whose real name was Robert Leroy Parker, was born in Utah in 1867, the grandson of a Mormon bishop. He took early to a life of crime and adopted the name 'Cassidy' in admiration of Mike Cassidy, a rustler

[161]

who taught him to shoot and steal livestock; he was dubbed 'Butch' after working for a short time in a butcher's shop.

By all accounts Butch was a likeable fellow; a Pinkerton wanted circular described him as having a 'cheerful and affable manner'. Although he packed a gun and was skilled in its use he was never known to kill anybody, and indeed it is claimed that he eschewed gratuitous violence. He used his quick wit and strength of character to dominate the other desperate members of the Wild Bunch.

Cassidy introduced an explosive element into the game of robbing trains; he used dynamite to blow open the express car and to crack the safe. Sometimes too much dynamite was used, with spectacular results. In June 1899 the Wild Bunch stopped the Union Pacific's Overland Flyer at

Express car blown apart by the Wild Bunch, who used too much dynamite to crack the safe.

Reward notice issued by the Union Pacific, dated 10 June 1899, for the Wild Bunch raiders.

$18,000.00
REWARD

€€

Union Pacific Railroad and Pacific Express Companies jointly, will pay $2,000.00 per head, dead or alive, for the six robbers who held up Union Pacific mail and express train ten miles west of Rock Creek Station, Albany County, Wyoming, on the morning of June 2nd, 1899.

The United States Government has also offered a reward of $1,000.00 per head, making in all $3,000.00 for each of these robbers.

Three of the gang described below, are now being pursued in northern Wyoming; the other three are not yet located, but doubtless soon will be.

DESCRIPTION: One man about 32 years of age; height, five feet, nine inches; weight 185 pounds; complexion and hair, light; eyes, light blue; peculiar nose, flattened at bridge and heavy at point; round, full, red face; bald forehead; walks slightly stooping; when last seen wore No. 8 cow-boy boots.

Two men, look like brothers, complexion, hair and eyes, very dark; larger one, age about 30; height, five feet, five inches; weight, 145 pounds; may have slight growth of whiskers; smaller one, age about 28; height, five feet, seven inches; weight 135 pounds; sometimes wears moustache.

Any information concerning these bandits should be promptly forwarded to Union Pacific Railroad Company and to the United States Marshal of Wyoming, at Cheyenne

UNION PACIFIC RAILROAD COMPANY.
PACIFIC EXPRESS COMPANY.

Omaha, Nebraska, June 10th, 1899

[163]

Posse which trailed the "Wild Bunch"

1. George Hiatt.
2. T. T. Kelliher, (now Chief Special Agent, I. C. R. R.)
3. Joe Lefores.
4. H. Davis.
5. Si Funk.
6. Jeff Carr.

Wilcox, Wyoming by placing a red danger lantern on the line. When the train halted, near a small wooden bridge, two of the highwaymen climbed into the engineer's car and ordered him to uncouple the engine and the express car from the rest of the train.

Having driven the double unit over the bridge, the bandits blew the latter up. When the messenger refused to open the door of the express car, the robbers blasted it open with a stick of dynamite. They then placed ten pounds of explosive on the safe (a sledge hammer to crack a nut), lit

The posse hired and transported by the Union Pacific to trail and hound the Wild Bunch. When things became too hot for them, Butch and the Sundance Kid left the United States for South America, where they continued their banditry.

[164]

the fuse and retired. The resulting big bang blew the safe apart and shattered the car, filling the air with a blizzard of paper money and bonds. The stunned outlaws gathered up the widely scattered notes and rode off with an estimated 30,000 dollars.

Butch Cassidy and the Wild Bunch were pursued by the Pinkerton agents and by special, train-borne posses (with their horses on board) organized by the Union Pacific. When things became too hot for them in the United States, Cassidy and the Sundance Kid (Harry Longbaugh) sailed to South America and continued their banditry there.

For years it was believed that they had died in a gun battle with government troops in Bolivia in 1909, but Cassidy's sister, Lula Parker Betenson has always insisted that Butch did not die in Bolivia but returned to the United States, visited his family in Utah, and settled down to a respectable life under an assumed name until he died in the 1930s. Mystery still cloaks the end of the Old West's most likeable bandit.

A Select Bibliography

AINSWORTH, HARRISON. *Rookwood*. London, 1834, often reprinted.

BARLOW, DEREK. *Dick Turpin and the Gregory Gang*. London, 1973.

BOURKE, FRANCIS. *Great American Train Robberies*. New York, 1909.

EARLE, ALICE MORSE. *Stagecoach & Tavern Days*. London, 1900, 1969.

EVANS, HILARY and MARY. *Hero on a Stolen Horse*. London, 1977.

HARPER, CHARLES G. *Half-Hours with the Highwaymen*. London, 1908.

HIBBERT, CHRISTOPHER. *Highwaymen*. London, 1967. *The Road to Tyburn*. London, 1957.

HORAN, JAMES D. *The Wild Bunch*. New York, 1958, 1970. *The Authentic Wild West: The Outlaws*. New York, 1977.

HOWSON, GERALD. *The Thief-Taker General*. London, 1970.

JACKSON, JOSEPH H. *Bad Company*. New York, 1939.

JOHNSON, CHARLES. *General History of the Most Famous Highwaymen*. London, 1734, often reprinted.

JOY, WILLIAM and PRIOR, TOM. *The Bushrangers*. London, 1971.

MAXWELL, G. S. *Highwaymen's Heath*. Hounslow, 1934, 1949.

OSBORNE, CHARLES. *Ned Kelly*. London, 1970.

POINTER, LARRY. *In Search of Butch Cassidy*. Norman, Oklahoma, 1977.

PRINGLE, PATRICK. *Stand and Deliver*. London, 1951.

SETTLE, WILLIAM A., JR. *Jesse James Was His Name*. Columbia, Missouri, 1966.

SMITH, ALEXANDER. *Complete History of the Most Notorious Highwaymen*. London, 1719, often reprinted.

[167]